CONTENTS

INTRODUCTION

I n August 1942 *Baseball Digest* was launched against all odds of success as its pulp pages hit newsstands during wartime shortages. Competing against established magazines already devoting themselves to America's pastime, *Baseball Digest* is the only one left standing more than three-quarters of a century later. Still beating the odds in today's digital world, it is the longest-running baseball magazine in the world.

"To be still around after 76 years is pretty amazing in itself," said former editor Bob Kuenster. "There is a lot of pride in that. We had a lot of people, and even some major league players, saying, 'My dad used to read *Baseball Digest* as a kid.'"

For nearly 50 years a Kuenster was at the helm of the magazine. Bob's father, John, who had covered both the Cubs and White Sox for the old *Chicago Daily News*, became editor in May 1969. Bob joined the magazine as an assistant editor right out of college in 1987 and became editor in 2012, the same year his father died. He held the post until 2018.

2012 was the magazine's 70th anniversary, and to mark the occasion the long-time black and white publication moved to full color with a fresh design. *Baseball Digest* also joined forces that

year with the scouting service Pro Scouting to bring its readers material previously available only to those deep inside the baseball industry.

However, the editorial feature most responsible for transforming the magazine from a simple digest of the best stories and reports from around baseball to what we read today was the inclusion of a segment called, The Game I'll Never Forget. Launched by the elder Kuenster in his first year as editor, it featured an account in each issue by a player, manager, broadcaster or umpire about his most enduring memory in baseball.

Fifty of those personal reflections are published in this book, and 32 of the speakers have made it all the way from those games into Cooperstown.

"It was an angle to give the fan some personality," Bob Kuenster said. "It started with announcers; the first three or four were broadcasters because they were used to telling stories."

Soon George Vass, an accomplished baseball and multi-discipline writer for the *Daily News* and then the *Chicago Sun-Times*, took over responsibility for interviewing the players, editing their comments and presenting them fully in the first person. It was a classic, as-told-to format.

Vass was followed by Barry Rozner, and later, among others, Bruce Levine

and Joel Bierig. In recent years The Game I'll Never Forget has evolved into a third-person story with ample quotes from the player whose memory is being featured. The handful of stories published in this style that are included in this book have been edited into a first-person narrative for consistency, using copious quotes from the third-person reportage. It's the way Vass built his stories.

"He was a fantastic writer," the younger Kuenster said of Vass.

The recollections harvested for this book span the 1950s to the 2000s. Both Duke Snider and Vin Scully recall the Brooklyn Dodgers' stunning World Series win over the New York Yankees in 1955 (even Yogi Berra can't help but touch on it as one of his worst memories). Stan "The Man" Musial describes in detail the day in 1958 that he collected his 3,000th hit. Carl Yastrzemski selects the final game of Boston's 1967 season, the "Impossible Dream," which not only put the Red Sox into the World Series for the first time in 21 years but would also make him baseball's only Triple Crown hitter for the next 45 years. Umpire Satch Davidson watched Hank Aaron touch home for his 715th home run, breaking The Babe's record, and also presided over the plate when Carlton Fisk danced his way into a waiting

THE BASEBALL GAME

I'LL NEVER FORGET

THE BASEBALL GAME
I'LL NEVER FORGET

EDITED BY
STEVE MILTON

Fifty Major Leaguers
Recall Their Finest Moments

FIREFLY BOOKS

A FIREFLY BOOK

Published by Firefly Books Ltd. 2018

First printing

Library of Congress Control Number: 2018938147

Library and Archives Canada Cataloguing in Publication
The baseball game I'll never forget : fifty major leaguers
recall their finest moments / edited by Steve Milton.
Includes index.
ISBN 978-0-228-10023-2 (softcover)
1. Baseball players--Anecdotes. 2. Baseball--Anecdotes.
I. Milton, Steve, editor
GV865.A1B38 2018   796.357092'2   C2018-901764-3

Published in the United States by
Firefly Books (U.S.) Inc.
P.O. Box 1338, Ellicott Station
Buffalo, New York 14205

Published in Canada by
Firefly Books Ltd.
50 Staples Avenue, Unit 1
Richmond Hill, Ontario L4B 0A7

Selected and edited by Steve Milton, with additional text by Steve Milton
Cover and interior design by Matt Filion

Printed in China

Canadä

We acknowledge the financial support of the Government of Canada.

Hank Aaron is carried from the field after his homer gave the Milwaukee Braves a 4–2 victory over the St. Louis Cardinals in the 11th inning to win the 1957 National League pennant.

Red Sox mob in the 12th inning of Game 6 in the 1975 World Series — a game widely viewed as the greatest ever played. Mike Piazza recalls the emotionally charged game he starred in at Shea Stadium on September 21, 2001. It was the first baseball game in New York after 9/11, and the players, Piazza in particular, felt its restorative impact.

Baseball is an individual game within a team game. As such, many of the memories recounted in these pages have a dual focus. Roberto Clemente was robbed of most of the satisfaction of his three-homer game in 1967 because his Pirates ended up losing the game. Tom Seaver of the New York Mets nearly recorded the first perfect game in franchise history, in 1969, but that story is a footnote to his team winning an important divisional matchup. Ken Griffey shrugs off the personal disappointment of his narrow miss on winning the batting title with the Cincinnati Reds in 1976 because his team wound up World Series champs that year.

Another thread that runs through these stories is the introspection that comes from playing a game mostly about failure. Andre Dawson ponders the nature of hitting in bunches; Snider, one of the greatest center fielders in history, references three years of insecurity with his play. The never flashy but amazingly consistent Rod Carew speaks about finally feeling accepted by the fans in Minnesota — 11 All-Star years into his time with the Twins. Even those who've thrown no-hitters, like Dave Stieb, stress that it takes an extraordinary amount of luck to pull off the feat. Maybe that's why Don Larsen seems so nonchalant in recollecting his World Series perfect game.

We'll end this introduction by going back to the beginning. John died four years before the Chicago Cubs won their first World Series since 1908, but he did live long enough to see the crosstown White Sox, a team he covered most of his life, win their first title in 88 years.

"The greatest game I ever went to was Game 2 of the World Series in 2005," his son Bob said. "Scott Podsednik hit a walkoff home run. At the time my dad was 80 and had never seen a Chicago World Series winner. The first thing that came to my mind was, 'No cheering in the press box.'

"Dad never cheered … but you could see the joy on his face."

For fans young and old, please enjoy this selection from "The Game I'll Never Forget."

— Steve Milton, 2018

WELCOME TO THE MAJORS

BROOKS ROBINSON
11

JUAN MARICHAL
14

BERT BLYLEVEN
19

BOB WELCH
22

FERNANDO VALENZUELA
26

JOHN LACKEY
28

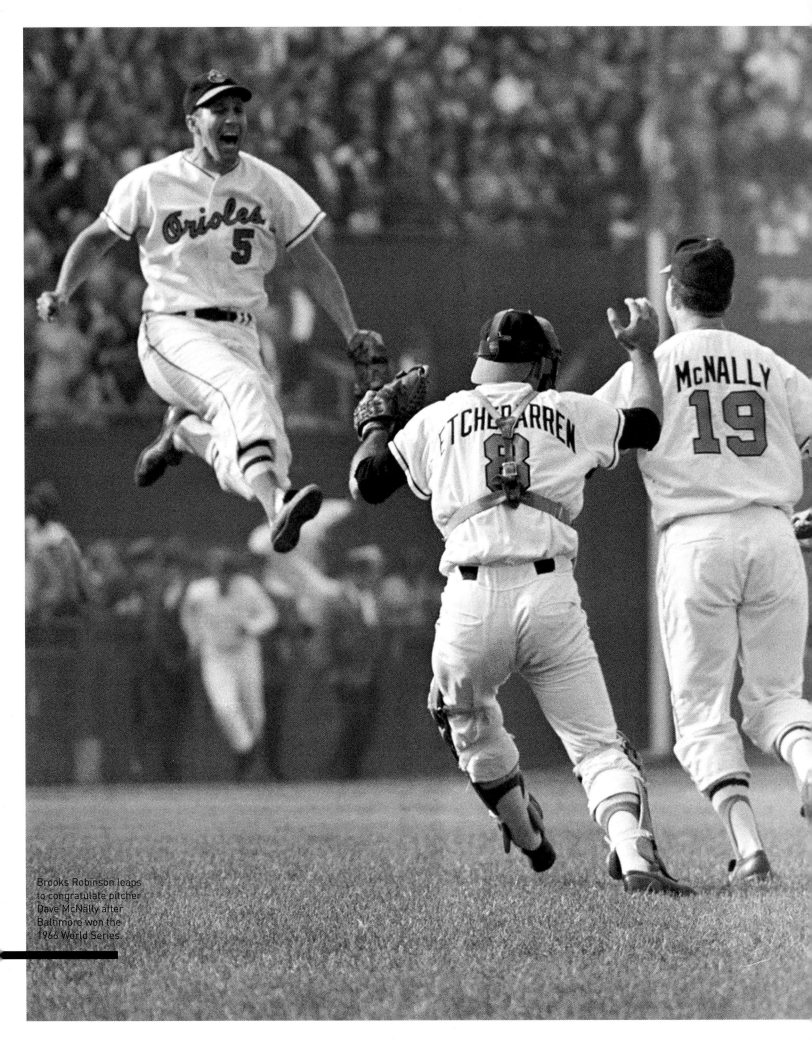

Brooks Robinson leaps
to congratulate pitcher
Dave McNally after
Baltimore won the
1966 World Series.

BROOKS ROBINSON
HUMBLE BEGINNINGS

SEPTEMBER 17, 1955

AS TOLD TO GEORGE VASS, *BASEBALL DIGEST*, OCTOBER 1972

It's illuminating to read how the greatest fielding third baseman in history succeeded immediately but then struggled. After his major league debut in 1955, described here, Brooks Robinson played only 70 more games over his first three seasons with the Baltimore Orioles. It wasn't until 1958 that he made the team and became a full-time player.

Called "Mr. Hoover" or the "Human Vacuum Cleaner," Robinson played 2,792 games at third base for the Orioles and fielded a phenomenal .971 at the hot corner, winning a record 16 consecutive Gold Gloves. He played a total of 2,896 games over his 23 seasons — all with Baltimore. Only Carl Yastrzemski, Hank Aaron and Stan Musial had played more games for one franchise.

When Robinson suited up for his first game in the majors, the Orioles were two years removed from being the sad-sack St. Louis Browns. The Orioles won two pennants with Robinson at third, their first in 1966, then again in 1970 when Robinson was World Series MVP. The Orioles won another World Series in 1983 — the year Robinson was elected to the Baseball Hall of Fame.

—SM

Brooks Robinson

1958 Topps; #307

3rd BASE   BALTIMORE ORIOLES

'll never forget the exciting days right before my graduation from Little Rock (Ark.) Senior High School in May 1955. Twelve of the 16 major league clubs back then were interested to varying degrees in signing me, and it was a lot of fun trying to decide which offer to take.

I'd just turned 18 a few days before graduation, and ever since I had been a little kid, all summer long I'd either practiced or played baseball. We didn't have a high school team, but an American Legion team filled the gap.

I played basketball on our high school team, and one year we went all the way to the semifinals in the state tournament. We lost by just one point to undefeated Jonesboro. I was good enough at basketball to be offered a scholarship by the University of Arkansas, so when the major league scouts came around, I was torn between going to college or trying to make it in baseball. Luckily, as it turned out, I chose baseball, and I've been fortunate enough to be successful in the game.

May 29, 1955, the day after graduation, was an exciting day. My dad and I weighed several offers, including one from the Orioles that included a $4,000 bonus. We slept on the offer, but the next morning I made my decision to sign with Baltimore, and I've never regretted it.

At the time the Orioles were a young team in a building program, and I figured I had a good chance to make the major leagues in three years, so I made that my goal.

Immediately after signing I went to Baltimore and spent two weeks with the Orioles just getting acquainted. I didn't get to play, but I did work out with the club and got to go on a road trip. The Orioles then sent me to York (Pa.), their Class-B farm team in the Piedmont League.

I got off to a good start in professional baseball. I hit .331 at York and felt I was making real progress. I felt even better about it when, after the Piedmont League season ended, the Orioles called me up to finish out the year with them.

Naturally I didn't figure I'd get much of a chance to play with them. Paul Richards, who was managing the Orioles at the time, had told me before sending me to York that he liked what he saw in me, but that I needed to get some more experience.

But I have to admit I was pretty excited when I got to Baltimore. I

BOXSCORE

	1	2	3	4	5	6	7	8	9	R	H	E
WASHINGTON SENATORS	0	0	0	0	1	0	0	0	0	1	10	2
BALTIMORE ORIOLES	0	1	1	0	0	0	0	1	X	3	10	1

went straight to Memorial Stadium because the Orioles were playing against the Washington Senators. I got into uniform and chose a good spot in the dugout to watch the game. I didn't figure on being anything other than a spectator.

I was just sitting there, minding my own business, when coach Lum Harris came over to me. I wasn't even thinking about getting in the lineup because Don Leppert was the regular third baseman. But Harris surprised me.

"Leppert's not feeling well," he said. "Get your glove, 'Robbie,' you're on third."

I was a little shaky as I went out to the infield to warm up. Looking back I guess it was a blessing that I didn't know the day before that I was going to play or I might not have slept all night. As it was, I was nervous just lobbing the ball back and forth with Gus Triandos, who was playing first base that day.

It was a real thrill though when they made the announcement over the loudspeaker: "Playing third base in place of Leppert, batting sixth, Brooks Robinson."

Eddie Lopat, who was finishing out his career, was our starting pitcher and Chuck Stobbs started for the Senators.

My heart was in my throat when Lopat threw the first pitch of the game to Eddie Yost, the leadoff man for Washington. I was concentrating so hard on Yost that I didn't even hear our shortstop, Willy Miranda, yelling at me to play nearer the bag.

The first time I went to bat, Stobbs got me to swing into a pitch that ended up as an easy grounder to the shortstop and I was thrown out by 10 feet. The second time up, in the fourth inning, I got hold of one and hit a clean shot over third base for a single. I can remember Mickey Vernon, the Senators first baseman, smiling at me when I came back to the bag after rounding first.

"Nice hit, kid," he said. "Welcome to the big leagues."

I got out the next time up, but in the eighth inning I came up with a man on second base. We were ahead 2–1 and I was thinking, Wouldn't that be something if could drive in a run in my first major league game and help win it!

Darned if I didn't get a single to drive in the run to put us ahead 3–1. I was really feeling good now, maybe a little cocky.

After the game I went to the phone and called my dad long distance to Little Rock.

"I went 2-for-4 and got a ribbie, Dad," I told him. "I'm here in the majors to stay. This is my cup of tea. I don't know what I was doing in the minors this year."

I talked too soon. I went 0-for-18 the rest of the season and struck out 10 times. Every time I struck out I thought about what I'd said to my dad.

I learned a good lesson, something I'll never forget.

JUAN MARICHAL
ONE-HIT WONDER

JULY 19, 1960

AS TOLD TO GEORGE VASS, *BASEBALL DIGEST*, JANUARY 1973

Juan Marichal was promoted to the San Francisco Giants at the beginning of the 1960s and became a central figure in the most dominant decade of pitching in baseball history. Marichal won more games than any other pitcher during the '60s. He won 20 games six times in the decade, including 25 twice ('63 and '66) and a career-high 26 in 1968.

Three years after his first major league game, described here, Marichal played in the "Greatest Game Ever Pitched," beating Milwaukee's Warren Spahn, 1–0. Both starters went the distance in the marathon game, which ended with Willie Mays' home run in the bottom of the 16th inning. Marichal struck out 10 Braves, and of the eight hits he allowed, all but one (a double by Spahn) were singles.

After he threw a one-hitter in his first major league start Marichal followed it up with two complete-game victories. He eventually finished 6-2 with a 2.66 ERA as a 22-year-old for a team that finished 16 games away from the pennant. His uncommonly high leg kick and threatening brush-back pitches made him one of the most intimidating pitchers of his era.

—SM

Juan Marichal of the
San Francisco Giants
in 1960

1961 Topps; #417

JUAN MARICHAL
Pitcher

San Francisco
Giants

In July 1960 I was supposed to pitch in the Pacific Coast League All-Star Game when Red Davis, our manager at Tacoma, came up to me. He had a funny little smile on his face. He said something, but I did not understand him at first. Finally it came to me what he was saying.

"Congratulations, Juan, you've been called up by the Giants. You're to leave for San Francisco. Forget about the All-Star Game. The Giants want you to report right away."

Naturally I was very excited. I thought maybe I would finish the season at Tacoma, but it was not so surprising that the Giants called me up because I was pitching good ball, going 11-5 in half a season.

Just before I was called up the Giants had fired Bill Rigney as manager and Tom Sheehan became the new boss. The only thing he told me when I reported to the club in San Francisco on July 10 was that I was going to pitch batting practice for a few days. He told me also to keep an eye on the opposition batters and learn something about them.

Eddie Logan, the clubhouse man, gave me No. 27, and I have worn it ever since.

All I did the first week was work out, pitch batting practice and watch the opposing hitters as Sheehan said I should. On July 19 he started me in a night game against the Philadelphia Phillies at Candlestick Park in San Francisco.

I was a little nervous when they announced my name. I felt funny. But as soon as I went to the mound everything was calm.

I didn't know the opposing players' names. Hobie Landrith, who was catching me, went over the Phillies hitters with me before the game, but we talked about them by numbers.

Later on I found out that the first two batters I faced, both of which I got out, were Ruben Amaro and Tony Taylor. They could really hit!

I retired the first six men to face me without trouble. My high kick delivery makes it difficult for hitters to pick up the pitches. I think that is especially true the first time a hitter has to face me.

In the second inning we got a run. Orlando Cepeda hit a double to start it out and Jim Davenport followed with a single to score him. We got another run in the fifth inning on singles by

JULY 19, 1960

BOXSCORE

	1	2	3	4	5	6	7	8	9	R	H	E
PHILADELPHIA PHILLIES	0	0	0	0	0	0	0	0	0	0	1	0
SAN FRANCISCO GIANTS	0	1	0	0	1	0	0	0	X	2	10	1

Don Blasingame and Willie Kirkland.

So we were ahead, 2–0, by the sixth inning, and the Phillies had yet to get a man on-base. I retired the side in the sixth and the first man up in the seventh.

I had retired 19 men in a row. Somebody — I don't remember who — made an error for us and the Phillies got their first runner on-base.

I got the next batter to fly out, and after a wild pitch and a walk I got another fly ball to retire the side.

I wasn't thinking about the no-hitter. As a matter of fact I didn't even know I was pitching one. Honest! Nobody told me about it. All I knew was that we were leading, 2–0, in the game.

The Phillies sent up Clay Dalrymple, a catcher, to pinch hit with two men out in the eighth. Landrith had told me about Dalrymple. "He's a good fastball hitter," he said, "so don't give him a good fastball to hit."

So the first pitch I threw Dalrymple was a curveball low. He lined it to center field for a single.

That was the only hit they got off me. I won the game, 2–0, and struck out 12 men. I had pitched a one-hitter in my first major league game.

The reporters were all around me after the game in the locker room. Somebody even mentioned Bobo Holloman, a pitcher who had pitched a no-hitter for the St. Louis Browns in his first major league start. I had never heard of him.

I had never even heard of Dalrymple, either, who had got the only hit off me after seven and two-thirds innings of no-hit ball. I just knew him by number when he came to bat and by what Landrith had told me about him.

I got to know him better during my career. He never seemed to have too much trouble hitting me. I just couldn't get him out consistently.

That game is the one I will never forget — my first game in the major leagues.

After that people started talking about my high kick and how it made it difficult for the batters to see the ball coming off the mound. They thought it must be hard for me to be a good fielder because of the way I delivered the ball. Maybe hitters could bunt on me.

But at the time it was not so easy for batters to bunt. I threw to make sure they couldn't.

Nobody bunted on me in that first game. Nobody could bunt what I threw.

After the game I remember Sheehan said, "All right. All right." That is all he could say.

It was all right.

BERT BLYLEVEN
A DEBUT TO REMEMBER

JUNE 5, 1970

AS TOLD TO GEORGE VASS, *BASEBALL DIGEST*, DECEMBER 1992

If Bert (born Rik Aalbert) Blyleven had faced Lee Maye near the end of his career rather than in his first appearance, he likely wouldn't have thrown him that fastball.

Over his career Blyleven, who was born in the Netherlands and spent three years in Canada before his family moved to California when he was five, became one of the greatest curveball pitchers in the history of the game. He had started only 21 minor league games when he faced Maye in the bottom of the first inning at Washington's RFK Stadium in his major league debut. He struck out seven and walked just one, and didn't allow an extra base hit after Maye rudely welcomed him to the big leagues.

Blyleven went on to pitch 22 years in the majors, half of those in Minnesota where he began his career in 1970. He won two World Series (one with the Pittsburgh Pirates in 1979 and the other during his second stint with the Twins in 1987) and finished his Hall of Fame career with 287 wins and 4,970 innings pitched. He's fifth on the all-time list in strikeouts and ninth in shutouts.

—SM

Bert Blyleven pitches for the Minnesota Twins in 1985.

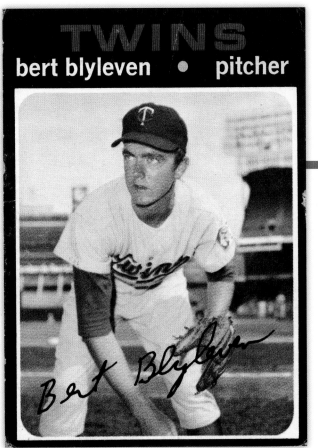

TWINS
bert blyleven • pitcher

1971 Topps; #26

 know for sure that when I made my first major league appearance in 1970, I didn't expect to be pitching more than 20 years later. It's almost mind-boggling the way the years have gone by and that I've been able to stay around for so long.

There have been a lot of highlights along the way, games that stand out in my memory for one reason or the other.

Naturally winning a playoff game or a World Series game is always something that is a highlight of your career. And I've been fortunate enough to do both, to pitch for a couple of World Series champions and win a game in each Series. Then there's the no-hitter I pitched against the California Angels for the Texas Rangers in 1977.

One thing that stands out about that no-hitter was that I'd been hurt for a couple weeks and that was my first start coming back. Normally you're not that sharp after being out two weeks, but I had good stuff in spite of having been laid off so long, and good control of my breaking pitch.

The year before I'd been traded by Minnesota to Texas and I remember my fourth and fifth starts for the Rangers were both 1–0 wins and both went 10 innings. In fact I won two more 1–0 games that season and lost a couple. It was just one of those stretches that's hard to explain when either nobody's hitting or everybody's pitching a great game.

And it all started in 1970 when I was called up by the Twins from Evansville in the minor leagues on June 1. I was only 19 years old and you can imagine how exciting that was. When you're that young and up for the first time naturally you wonder if you belong in the big leagues. As a kid, I'd always dreamed of pitching in the major leagues, and now I had the chance. That's what makes my first big league start probably the most important game of my career.

When I reported to the Twins, manager Bill Rigney told me to sit next to him on the bench and that I'd be starting against Washington a few days later. We were in first place at that time, so that really was something to think about.

I was really nervous that Friday. I got to the ballpark in Washington about 3 p.m. and my legs were shaking, wondering if I'd be up to my first start in the major leagues. I had plenty of

BOXSCORE

	1	2	3	4	5	6	7	8	9	R	H	E
MINNESOTA TWINS	1	0	0	0	1	0	0	0	0	2	8	0
WASHINGTON SENATORS	1	0	0	0	0	0	0	0	0	1	5	0

time to think about it because it was a night game.

Most rookies probably feel the way I did, wondering if they're really capable of being a major leaguer. Being only 19 probably made that feeling of doubt all the more intense.

Before the game George Mitterwald, the catcher, went over all the hitters with me to let me know how he thought I should pitch to them.

The first major league batter I faced was Lee Maye, a pretty good hitter. The count got up to 3-2 and Mitterwald signaled for a fastball. I had a pretty good fastball at the time, so I thought I'd challenge him and throw it right over the plate. Well, Maye got all of it, hitting it about 400 feet over the right-field wall.

What a feeling! The first major league batter I'd faced and he'd hit a home run. I was dejected and mad, both at myself and at Mitterwald for calling the pitch. Being a rookie I had

to throw it, but when you're 19…

I caught sight of Rigney in the dugout and to my surprise he was smiling. Welcome to the big leagues, kid, he seemed to be saying. That helped settle me down, and I got the side out. When I got back to the dugout Rigney told me just to relax and stay calm.

The home run seemed to help me get over my nervousness. We'd scored in the first, so we were in a tie game and I was able to mentally start over and focus on pitching a good game.

I shut the Senators out the next six innings, and in the fifth I even laid down a sacrifice bunt to move what proved to be the winning run to second base. We won the game, 2–1, with Ron Perranoski coming in to pitch the last two innings and save the win for me.

I'd won my first major league start.

I was so happy after the game and called home to talk to my parents. What my dad wanted to know was

how I'd done against Frank Howard, the Senators' big slugger. I told him Howard didn't get a hit and I'd struck him out once. That made my dad happy.

Looking back I think that first major league appearance probably was the most important game of my career. It convinced me — and my dad — that I belonged in the big leagues.

> I WAS REALLY NERVOUS THAT FRIDAY. I GOT TO THE BALLPARK IN WASHINGTON ABOUT 3 P.M. AND MY LEGS WERE SHAKING . . .

BOB WELCH
ROOKIE VS. REGGIE

OCTOBER 11, 1978

AS TOLD TO GEORGE VASS, *BASEBALL DIGEST*, SEPTEMBER 1991

No major league pitcher has won 25 games or more since Bob Welch put up 27 for the 1990 Oakland Athletics. And nobody before Welch had won 27 since Steve Carlton did it with the Philadelphia Phillies 18 years earlier.

Welch spent his first 10 seasons with the Los Angeles Dodgers before being traded to Oakland, where he enjoyed his greatest success. He won 17 games in his first two seasons with the A's — the highest win totals of his career outside of 1990 when he beat out Roger Clemens and teammate Dave Stewart to capture the Cy Young Award. He won 211 games over the course of his career, but he never did win a World Series game, going 0-1 in three starts, though he was 3-2 in six league championship series over his 17 seasons in the majors.

Welch was just a 21-year-old rookie with the Dodgers in the 1978 World Series versus the New York Yankees when he outdueled "Mr. October" himself, Reggie Jackson, in one of the most memorable strikeouts in franchise history. He captures the tenseness of that classic confrontation here.

—SM

Bob Welch delivers a pitch for the Los Angeles Dodgers in 1986.

1979 Topps; #318

BOB WELCH P
DODGERS

When I was a kid growing up in Detroit, I loved the Tigers. They were my team, a bunch of old pros that won the 1968 World Series. Al Kaline, Dick McAuliffe, Norm Cash, Willie Horton — they were my heroes, and they played hard.

They were competitors. My favorite was Mickey Lolich, a fat pitcher, who was the hero of the '68 World Series. I was 11 years old then, and it was Lolich's performance that put the idea in my head that I wanted to pitch in the major leagues.

When I first came up to the majors, like most young pitchers I didn't know all that much about pitching. I just threw the ball hard. I was always hyperactive as a kid, and especially in my early years as a major league pitcher. I couldn't sit still. I was impatient and in a hurry. I guess it was my competitiveness.

That edge can be a great advantage, but it also can be a weakness. You tend to concentrate so much on what's directly in front of you that you lose sight of the overall picture. You don't take time to think. When I was younger, I'd start knocking heads with a batter and the next thing I knew three runs were in. I had to learn to slow down and take more time. If you do that, you might give someone time to make a play.

That's the biggest thing I've learned over my career: you need to get ready to pitch mentally, game by game and during the course of a game. I think that change in approach has helped me with my consistency over the past few years.

I've been fortunate enough to pitch for some good teams with the Los Angeles Dodgers and the Oakland A's. As far as career highs go, winning 27 games was great, but nothing can top the opportunity of pitching in a league championship series or a World Series, and luckily I've had a lot of those.

One thing that has escaped me over the years, though, is being the winning pitcher in a World Series game. In 1989 I was supposed to start the third game of the World Series for the A's against the San Francisco Giants, but there was that terrible earthquake just before the game. When a tragedy like that happens you can't worry about the World Series. When it resumed 10 days later the rotation was rested and I never did get a start. We won Games 3 and 4 for the sweep.

OCTOBER 11, 1978

BOXSCORE

	1	2	3	4	5	6	7	8	9	R	H	E
NEW YORK YANKEES	0	0	2	0	0	0	1	0	0	3	11	0
LOS ANGELES DODGERS	0	0	0	1	0	3	0	0	X	4	7	0

The game most people remind me about, though, is the one in 1978 when I came out of the bullpen for the ninth inning in the second game of the World Series in L.A. The Dodgers had called me up in June from Albuquerque and I'd had some success starting (7-4). There was talk I'd start the fourth game of the World Series against the New York Yankees, but in the second game they told me to stay in the bullpen in case I was needed.

We'd won the series opener and in Game 2 we were leading by a run, 4–3, in the ninth inning. Burt Hooton had pitched the first six innings for us and Terry Forster had taken us into the ninth.

I was throwing nice and easy in the bullpen when Bucky Dent got a single and Paul Blair walked with one out. Thurman Munson and Reggie Jackson, the Yankees' best hitters, were the next two batters. That's when I was told

(manager) Tom Lasorda wanted me.

I was nervous, but in a good way. I just wanted to get in there and get it over with. When I got to the mound (second baseman) Davey Lopes told me, "Just throw your pitch," and Lasorda said, "Just throw strikes." And that's what I wanted to do — throw my fastball past 'em and get it over with.

Munson hit a fastball hard, a line drive, but it was right at Reggie Smith in right field. That made it two out and men on first and second with Jackson coming up.

I knew all about his reputation for getting the big hit. He'd already driven in all three runs for the Yankees in the game. But I wasn't scared. I just figured I'd blow it by him. I discovered it wasn't that easy, though. It took seven minutes, I was told afterward.

He could have killed the first pitch. It was over the plate and too low. But he swung and missed. The next one

was under his chin, though not on purpose, it just happened. He hit the dirt and dug back into the batter's box.

Jackson fouled back the next three pitches and then I threw a ball that was way inside. That made it six pitches, and he fouled off the seventh.

By this time the crowd was roaring. I tried to shut them out, to concentrate. I just wanted to get that third strike past him. That's all I had in mind. But the eighth pitch was high and inside to make it a full count, which meant the runners would be moving on the next pitch.

It seemed like his at-bat had gone on forever when I threw the ninth pitch to Jackson. He swung and missed. It was over. We'd won, 4–3.

That confrontation between Jackson and me has been talked about more than anything else I've been involved in in baseball. I know it's something I'll never be allowed to forget.

FERNANDO VALENZUELA

FEVER PITCH

OCTOBER 23, 1981

AS TOLD TO GEORGE VASS, *BASEBALL DIGEST*, JULY 1994

In his 17-year career Fernando Valenzuela played for six different teams, but the average baseball fan remembers him with only one of them.

Baseball has rarely seen anything like the "Fernandomania" that swept southern California in 1981 when the 20-year-old, who came to be called "El Toro," pitched his first full season for the Los Angeles Dodgers. With only 17.1 innings of major league pitching under his belt, Valenzuela was pressed into service as the 1981 Opening Day starter at Dodger Stadium because Jerry Reuss was hurt. He pitched a 2–0 shutout over the Houston Astros and proceeded to go 8-0, with four more shutouts, to start the season. He ended it by pitching in the World Series he recalls here. He was named both the National League Rookie of the Year and the Cy Young winner.

It was in the Dodgers' minor league system in Double-A where Valenzuela was taught to throw the screwball. It became his calling card over the course of his career. He played 11 years in Los Angeles, winning a career-best 21 games in 1986 and throwing a no-hitter against the St. Louis Cardinals at Dodger Stadium in 1990, his last season in L.A.

—SM

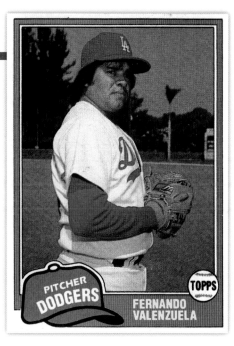

1981 Topps; #805T

When you're 20 years old and it's your first full year in the major leagues you don't think about what is going to stand out in your mind someday. You think, maybe, it's going to go on forever, that you are going to play baseball until you are very old. Then, maybe, you are going to sit back in the sun and tell your grandchildren about what you did.

When I first came to the Dodgers it was like a dream. Everything in this country was new to me and I couldn't speak English, but everybody was good to me, and I quickly felt like I was at home. I had confidence. I just liked to pitch and do the best I could for my team. It didn't surprise me — well, maybe a little — that I should have so much success in my first full season with the club.

I was very happy to pitch a no-hitter. Every pitcher is looking to throw one in his career. What made my no-hit game even more special was that before I took the mound I was watching TV in the clubhouse and saw Dave Stewart (of the Oakland Athletics) pitch a no-hitter against the Toronto Blue Jays. I told the guys, "You've seen one on TV. Now come

watch one live." Then I went out and pitched the no-hitter. Of course, I was just kidding before the game. Still, you remember something like that.

Another game I remember is the 1986 All-Star Game in Houston when I struck out five batters in a row, something they told me had been done only once, a long time before (1934) by Carl Hubbell. Winning my 20th game in '86 is also a personal highlight.

But the one I remember most is the World Series win I had in 1981. It was an important game; we'd lost the first two games to the New York Yankees and people were saying that it was all over. Not many teams lose the first two games of the World Series and come back to win.

I remember there was an earthquake in Los Angeles the morning before I was due to pitch in Game 3. It was not a big one, but you could feel it.

We scored three runs in the first inning, and when you've got an early lead like that it usually makes it easier on a pitcher. But then the Yankees started to hit the ball. I thought the earthquake came during the game they were hitting it so hard. I didn't have my best stuff and I was wild early

in the game. Pretty soon the Yankees were ahead, 4–3.

In the fifth inning we tied the game 4–4 and the bases were loaded with Mike Scioscia at bat for us. Tommy Lasorda came over to me and said in Spanish, "If we don't get the go-ahead run here, you're gone." Meaning he was going to pinch hit for me.

But then we scored the go-ahead run and Tommy left me in the game. I pitched well the next four innings and we won. We went on to win the next three games and the World Series after losing the first two.

It might not have been my best game as a pitcher, but it was a great game to win.

OCTOBER 23, 1981
BOXSCORE

	1	2	3	4	5	6	7	8	9	R	H	E
NEW YORK YANKEES	0	2	2	0	0	0	0	0	0	4	9	0
LOS ANGELES DODGERS	3	0	0	0	2	0	0	0	X	5	11	1

JOHN LACKEY
ROOKIE RESOLVE

OCTOBER 27, 2002

AS TOLD TO BARRY ROZNER, *BASEBALL DIGEST*, MAY 2016

Until John Lackey started Game 7 of the 2002 World Series, only one rookie had ever won a seventh game in the Fall Classic. That was Babe Adams, 93 years earlier.

Lackey had been up with Anaheim for only four months after pitching for the Angels' Triple-A club in Utah until late June. He went 9-4, got some relief action for the wild-card Angels against the New York Yankees and pitched a brilliant seven innings to beat Minnesota's Brad Radke in Game 4 of the ALCS.

The Angels had never been in a World Series until the 2002 tilt against the San Francisco Giants, and they had to rally from a 5–0 deficit in the seventh inning of Game 6 to stay alive. Lackey appeared in relief in Game 2, had a no-decision as the starter in Game 4 and got the ball again to start Game 7 when Ramon Ortiz came up with a sore wrist. Lackey went five innings for the 4–1 win, and Garret Anderson's bases-loaded double in the third inning provided the margin of victory.

Lackey would also win the Series-clinching Game 6 for the Boston Red Sox over the St. Louis Cardinals in 2013.

—SM

2002 Topps Heritage; #228

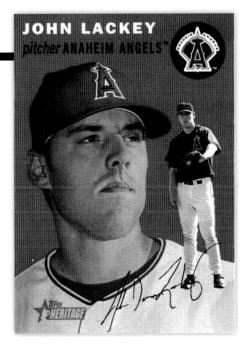

JOHN LACKEY
pitcher **ANAHEIM ANGELS**™

During the 2001 World Series I was sitting on my couch in Texas, watching Arizona and New York. I was thinking the same thing I always did: Will I ever get a chance to be on the mound in the World Series? What would it feel like to be on the mound for Game 7? I don't think there's a kid in America that doesn't dream about a situation like that at some point.

Then the very next year I was in the postseason. In Game 4 of the ALCS I pitched against Minnesota, and Brad Radke threw an incredible game. He was just lights out. It was a lot of fun because I was really dialed in, too. I wanted to match him out-for-out and inning-for-inning. I had to because he wasn't allowing anything.

But I also knew if I could keep us in it, our guys would get it done. It's what we did all year.

The guys were so good in the late innings. We were never out of a game, and it's something that was really alive on our bench every night. We always had a chance no matter what the score was, so as a pitcher you knew you just had to give them a chance.

I was a rookie and we had a team dominated by veterans. Our bullpen was outstanding, so I knew my job was to keep us in the game, get through five or six innings and then let the guys down in the bullpen do their jobs. It was a good formula.

When we were down 5–0 in Game 6 of the World Series, I'm sure the outside world thought we were done, but we knew we had nine outs left and that was a lot for our team to work with. We had great belief in our offense and in our bullpen, and we never felt like there was a game we couldn't win late.

Of course, I was nervous when I was given the start in Game 7, but I wasn't scared. I wasn't intimidated. It was fun. In that moment you just have to focus on executing as you always do and not let the moment become bigger than the pitch.

I was locating my fastball really well early, throwing in and setting up pitches away. When you can get that going early it helps with confidence. Then you just let it fly.

When Anderson hit his double in the third to put us up, it was the first time I felt the butterflies and I had to get control of myself again. That's when you have to be careful not to get ahead of yourself. I just calmed myself down and reminded myself to make pitches. That's all, just make pitches. One at a time.

In the fourth, when they got two on I figured I had one more inning, so I was really concentrating on every pitch. I put everything I had into those pitches and just made sure to execute. When the bullpen took over I tried not to sit there counting outs. But that's what I did, and when Troy Percival got Kenny Lofton to fly to center for the final out it felt like the ball was in the air forever. You can't believe how long it takes to come down. Your heart is pounding. You don't hear anything. You hold your breath.

And then we were World Series champions. It was a dream come true.

OCTOBER 27, 2002
BOXSCORE

	1	2	3	4	5	6	7	8	9	R	H	E
SAN FRANCISCO GIANTS	0	1	0	0	0	0	0	0	0	1	6	0
ANAHEIM ANGELS	0	1	3	0	0	0	0	0	X	4	5	0

CLUTCH HITTING

✕

YOGI BERRA
33

WILLIE MAYS
36

ROBERTO CLEMENTE
41

REGGIE JACKSON
44

ROD CAREW
49

BUCKY DENT
52

GEORGE BRETT
56

RYNE SANDBERG
59

ANDRE DAWSON
62

DAVE HENDERSON
65

TIM RAINES
68

JOE GIRARDI
70

Yogi Berra strokes a hit for the powerhouse Yankees in 1955.

YOGI BERRA
KNOCKING OUT 'NEWK'

OCTOBER 10, 1956

AS TOLD TO GEORGE VASS, *BASEBALL DIGEST*, DECEMBER 1971

*Because of his positional versatility and legendary malapropisms —
"Nobody goes there anymore, it's too crowded" — and long, colorful,
post-playing career as a manager and coach, it's easy to forget that
Yogi Berra is one of the best catchers in baseball history.*

   *Much of his career was spent behind the plate with the Yankees
juggernaut from the 1950s to mid-1960s, and he holds the all-time
record of 10 World Series championships as a player. Berra was a
clutch hitter with good plate coverage. And despite his 5-foot-7 stature
he could also hit for power and drive in runs. He had 358 homers and
1,430 RBIs in his 19-year playing career, which ended following four
games with the crosstown Mets in 1965 — the season after he took
the Yankees to the American League pennant as manager.*

   *Berra is one of only four catchers to field 1.000 in a season (1958)
and is one of only five players to win the American League MVP
award three times. He also played a strong left field later in his career.*

   *As a surprisingly balanced observer he even felt compelled here to
touch on his worst memory before recalling his greatest, both against
the Brooklyn Dodgers.*

—SM

1956 Topps; #110

YOGI BERRA

catcher NEW YORK YANKEES

When I start thinking about a game I'll never forget I have to remember a bad one as well as the good ones. A lot of times the bad things that happen are easier to remember than the good things.

You'll know what I mean when I mention the last game of the 1955 World Series. That's the one the Brooklyn Dodgers won to beat us New York Yankees.

They were leading us, 2–0, in the seventh game, and Johnny Podres was pitching really well when we came up in the sixth inning. We got a good rally going when Billy Martin walked and Gil McDougald beat out a bunt for a single. I was the next batter.

The Dodgers had made a change in the lineup before the inning had started. Don Zimmer had been playing second base, but George Shuba had batted for him. So when we came to bat the Dodgers moved "Junior" Gilliam from left field to second base, putting Sandy Amoros in left.

Amoros was playing me toward center, giving me a lot of room down the line. I hit a high fly ball down the line, though not well, and it looked like it might drop in and go for a double or triple. But Amoros came running over and grabbed the ball just a few feet off the ground.

He was able to get the ball over to first and double up McDougald and that killed the inning. Instead of two runs in and maybe a runner on third, we had two out. The Dodgers went on to win the game and the World Series.

I've wondered what would have happened if Gilliam had still been in left. He was right-handed and I don't think he could have caught that ball like Amoros, who had the glove on his right hand and could reach out for it, being left-handed.

Anyway, that was the bad one I remember.

Choosing the good one isn't all that easy. I caught Allie Reynolds when he pitched two no-hitters, and I played a lot of games that meant something because we won a lot of pennants with the Yankees. Naturally there were a lot of World Series games, too.

I was also the guy who caught Don Larsen when he pitched the perfect game in the 1956 Series. A catcher gets a lot of satisfaction when his pitcher does well. I can still remember the end of that game when Dale Mitchell struck out and I ran out to Larsen and jumped all over him. I've got to remember it since I've seen the rerun often enough on TV.

You can't top that perfect game too easily, but there is another game that's

OCTOBER 10, 1956

BOXSCORE

	1	2	3	4	5	6	7	8	9	R	H	E
NEW YORK YANKEES	2	0	2	1	0	0	4	0	0	9	10	0
BROOKLYN DODGERS	0	0	0	0	0	0	0	0	0	0	3	1

got to be the one I'll never forget, and it's from the same year. That's the last game of that 1956 World Series against the Dodgers in which I got some big hits.

Just like the year before, each team had won three games in the Series. Johnny Kucks started for us and the Dodgers had Don Newcombe going. "Newk" was a great pitcher, but he always had tough luck against us.

I didn't help Newk any. He'd pitched the second game of the Series, and I came up in the second inning with the bases loaded and hit a home run. That was the end of Newk in that game, though we didn't win it. Everybody was hitting that day and the Dodgers finally won, 13–8.

But this seventh game was different. This was the one that counted and we weren't forgetting how the Dodgers had beaten us the year before. I know I

could still remember Amoros making that catch.

Kucks was really good that game. He had everything working and the ball was going right where he wanted it. The Dodgers had just three hits and he only walked three.

Newk looked like he'd have a good day, too. His fastball looked good even after Hank Bauer singled to start the game. Hank stole second but Newk had struck out Billy Martin and Mickey Mantle when I came up.

Well, I got lucky and I hit the ball well. It went over the right-field fence to give us a two-run lead. I don't remember exactly, but I think it was a fastball waist high. Maybe Newk took a little off of it.

Newk got through the second inning all right, but he got into some trouble again in the third when Martin got a single with one out. I was

watching Newk, waiting for my turn at bat, and I thought he might work out of it.

He ripped a third strike by Mantle. That ball had steam on it. You don't fool Mickey easily. But when I went up there Newk must have lost a little. All I know is that this time I hit the ball and it went over the right-field scoreboard to make it 4–0. It was my third home run off him in that Series.

The grand slam and two more homers — that's eight runs off Newk in the Series batted in right there.

My second home run finished Newk and we got two more homers that day, by Ellie Howard and "Moose" Skowron, the last with the bases loaded. We took the seventh game 9–0 and won the Series.

That's the game I'll never forget. I always did hit Newk pretty well.

WILLIE MAYS
MAKING CONTACT

APRIL 30, 1961

AS TOLD TO GEORGE VASS, *BASEBALL DIGEST*, FEBRUARY 1974

Willie Mays, the "Say Hey Kid," was the ultimate five-tool player, patroling center field for the New York Giants in the 1950s and then for the San Francisco Giants when the franchise moved out west in 1958.

In the 1961 season he refers to here, his 40 home runs were second in the National League behind teammate Orlando Cepeda. That year Mays led the league in runs scored (129), finished third in RBIs (123), fifth in stolen bases (18) and tied for fourth among center fielders with seven assists.

That '61 season the American League expanded by two teams and Roger Maris and Mickey Mantle led the charge on Babe Ruth's 60-home run record. The National League would not expand, and thus not thin its pitching depth, until 1962, the year Mays had a career-high 141 RBIs.

In this anecdote Mays, a 20-time All-Star and two-time MVP, recalls sharing a room, and some disagreeable food, with Willie McCovey, the 1969 National League MVP. His four-homer game that followed — his most indelible baseball memory — came in the last of a three-game weekend series on the road against the Braves.

—SM

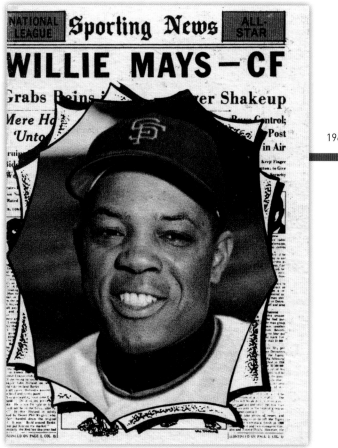

1961 Topps; #579

People suppose — maybe because there's been so much talk about it and they've shown it so much on TV — that my greatest thrill in baseball was the time I made that catch on Vic Wertz in the 1954 World Series. I'm not saying it wasn't a great thrill because it was, and so was winning that Series.

There have been a lot of other big thrills for me playing baseball, as most people know, seeing I was lucky enough to be out there so long and with such good teams.

Heck, what more of a thrill can there be than seeing Bobby Thomson hit that home run against the Brooklyn Dodgers in 1951 to win the pennant for us. I was in the on-deck circle waiting my turn at bat when he did it.

But no matter what game or play people remind me of when they ask if it was my biggest thrill, I always tell them the game in which I hit four home runs — that's the one.

It happened in Milwaukee on April 30, 1961, a Sunday, and it was the wildest game I was ever in…for home runs. We hit eight in that game and the Braves had a couple, with Hank Aaron hitting both of theirs.

That's 10 home runs in a game. You're not going to see that more than once or twice in a lifetime. I know I haven't and I'd never done anything like that four home run game before or since. I call it the greatest day of my baseball career.

More than how I hit those four home runs that day, what I remember are the things that happened during the couple days before.

I wasn't hitting at all in Milwaukee leading up to the final game of the series. I was in a slump, and I thought it was getting deeper. The funny thing is my team got 15 hits in the second game, Saturday, five of them home runs, but I didn't get any of them. And I didn't have any hits the first game, Friday, so I was 0-for-7 in the series.

Not only had I not had a hit in the first two games, but I hadn't hit one ball well at all.

I don't say I was feeling bad about the way I was going. But I was thinking about what to do to get out of what some people might call a slump.

APRIL 30, 1961

BOXSCORE

	1	2	3	4	5	6	7	8	9	R	H	E
SAN FRANCISCO GIANTS	1	0	3	3	0	4	0	3	0	14	14	0
MILWAUKEE BRAVES	3	0	0	0	0	1	0	0	0	4	8	1

Saturday night I had a chance to talk it over with (former manager) Leo Durocher, and he suggested a few things I might be doing wrong — gripping my bat, my stance, and so on. That made me feel a little better. Leo, who wasn't with the Giants by then, always could help me and I figured things would pick up.

Then I got sick. I was rooming with Willie McCovey at the time and he brought a double order of spareribs to the room. They tasted good, but an hour later I felt like somebody had kicked me in the stomach. I was so sick I had McCovey call the trainer up to the room and he gave me some medicine to settle my stomach. After a while I felt better and fell asleep.

In the morning I wasn't sure I'd be able to play that day. I felt weak as a cat. I figured I'd see how I was before the game and decide.

Batting practice wasn't too bad. I could get the bat around even if I didn't feel really strong. You never can tell, but I thought, "I might just get four hits today."

Lew Burdette, a right-hander, was pitching for the Braves. But I could always hit right-handers, so that didn't bother me. We had Billy Loes pitching, and he never had an easier day. We won 14–4.

Now, I can't remember what happened on every pitch that day. All I remember is that I hit the ball well every time I got the wood on it.

In the first inning I hit a home run to straightaway center. They say it went 420 feet. Nobody was on-base. In the third inning there was one man on, and this time I hit a pitch by Burdette some 400 feet into the stands in left-center.

In the fifth inning, Moe Drabowsky was now pitching for Milwaukee. I hit the ball well again, but it was right at the center fielder, Aaron.

The next time up, in the sixth inning, Seth Morehead was pitching and there were two men on. I hit the ball to deep left center. They say it went 450 feet. Up to that time I think I'd hit only one ball harder in my life. That was in old Sportsman's Park in St. Louis.

I was 3-for-4 with three home runs, and when I came to bat again in the eighth inning with a man on-base I think some of the Milwaukee fans were pulling for me to hit that fourth homer. It came off Don McMahon, who later pitched for the Giants. They say it went 430 feet.

Four home runs and eight runs batted in. I almost had a chance to make it more. The crowd was cheering for me to get another chance at bat in the ninth. I was in the on-deck circle with two out, but Jim Davenport grounded out, so I didn't get to try for the fifth home run.

I was just up there swinging. The pitches were in there and I just connected. What more can you say about my four home run day?

Roberto Clemente
in 1968.

ROBERTO CLEMENTE

HOMER HEAVEN

MAY 15, 1967

AS TOLD TO GEORGE VASS, *BASEBALL DIGEST*, SEPTEMBER 1971

The Pittsburgh Pirate's Roberto Clemente had only just turned 37 when he talked about his three-homer, seven-RBI game, but he would live to play only one more season.

A year after winning the 1971 World Series, Pittsburgh won the NL East and Clemente registered the 3,000th hit of his career on his final at-bat of the 1972 regular season. The Cincinnati Reds put an end to Pittsburgh's hopes for a second straight World Series title and that was the last baseball saw of Clemente. On New Year's Eve in '72 Clemente died in a plane crash while on his way to deliver humanitarian aid to earthquake survivors in Nicaragua.

Clemente routinely hit .300, which he did in 12 of the last 13 seasons of his 18-year major league career. His only miss during that stretch was the .291 he hit in 1968. He won the National League batting title four times and was league MVP in 1966, the year before the game he refers to in this flashback. Born in Puerto Rico he was the first Latin American to be a league MVP, to win a World Series as a starter (1960 and 1971) and to make the Hall of Fame.

—SM

BOB CLEMENTE • OUTFIELD

1967 Topps; #400

PIRATE

One game sticks out in my mind, not that there aren't any other big ones to remember. There are a lot of those, but this is the one I'll never forget because I did so well and yet we did not win.

I've said it many times and I still feel the same way about it: I never go for home runs. I go for hits because I don't believe that a good hitter hits .300 one year and drops to .200 the next. Either you're a good hitter or you are not — unless something is wrong with you physically, like when I hurt my back in 1957 and hit only .253 after I hit .311 the year before. But if you're a .300 hitter and you're healthy, you should hit.

I don't go for home runs because it is not the way to maintain a .300 average. The only thing I really think about in hitting is staying strong. If I stay strong I don't have to think about hitting.

When the 1967 season started I felt strong and I hit more home runs than I usually do. Not because I tried to, but because I hit the ball well and more of them happened to go out of the park. The team was going well after the first month of the 1967 season, and when we went into Cincinnati for a three-game series in mid-May we were right behind the Reds, who were in first place.

I was still feeling strong, early in the season, and when we went into Cincinnati I think I was hitting .370. At my age now — and even

then, when I was 32 — you come to a point where you get tired in the warmer weather. When you are 28 you feel good all the time, but at my age sometimes you feel groggy.

That game being in May the weather was still cool and I know I felt strong in Cincinnati. It was a night game and the Reds started Milt Pappas, a good pitcher.

In the first inning Maury Wills, who was playing shortstop for us that year, got on-base and I came up with one man out. I got around on an outside pitch by Pappas and hit it over the right-field fence in old Crosley Field for my first home run of the game.

I don't remember what I did for my next time at bat — all I know is that I got out. But my third time up, in the fifth inning, Wills was on-base again and this time I hit the ball over the center-field fence, which was a long way in the old Cincinnati park.

That was two home runs off Pappas and we were ahead, 4–0. It was nothing to excite me since I had hit two home

BOXSCORE

	1	2	3	4	5	6	7	8	9	10	R	H	E
PITTSBURGH PIRATES	2	0	0	0	2	0	2	0	1	0	7	8	1
CINCINNATI REDS	0	0	0	0	0	3	2	0	2	1	8	13	1

runs in a game before. Nothing I do well ever excites me. The only time I get happy is winning a game. And this game was not yet won.

The Reds scored three runs in the sixth inning, so the game was close again. But this was a good day for me, and in the seventh inning I came to bat with two men on-base. Darrell Osteen was now pitching for the Reds. I hit the ball well again, this time off the fence for a double to drive in two more runs.

Now I had six runs batted in and we were leading, 6–3. But the Reds were able to get to Pete Mikkelsen, who'd taken over for our starter, Bob Veale. They knocked Mikkelsen out in the seventh inning when they got two runs, and we were ahead by one run, 6–5, going into the ninth inning.

By this time Gerry Arrigo was pitching for the Reds. He got the first two men out in the ninth, so I came up to bat for the fifth time with nobody on-base. This time I hit the ball over the center-field fence again to give us a 7–5 lead.

I have to admit I was excited about what I had just done. I had never hit three home runs in a game before and this was something to remember: three home runs, a double and I had driven in all seven runs.

We were still leading 7–5 when the Reds came to bat in the last of the ninth, but they wouldn't let us win. Tony Perez got a hit and then Lee May hit a home run with one out to tie the game 7–7.

With the score tied and nobody on-base the Reds' manager let the pitcher, Arrigo, bat for himself. He hit it hard down the right-field line and it looked for a minute like the ball was going to go over the fence for a home run to win the game.

I got back quickly in right field, all the way to the fence. I wasn't sure I could reach the ball, but I went up and I saved the home run. I didn't catch the ball, but I knocked it down with my glove and it was a double. Luckily we got the side out and went into extra innings.

I thought we still had a chance to win, and maybe I could get another chance to bat. But that wasn't to be. In the bottom of the 10th inning Perez hit a double to center field to score Pete Rose and win the game 8–7, and that robbed me of most of the satisfaction I had from my performance. It was the biggest day I had ever had, and it had to come in a game that we lost.

A couple years later I again hit three home runs in a game, but that does not stick out in my mind like the one that we lost to Cincinnati. Doing so well and then losing — it was a strange feeling.

> . . . I DON'T BELIEVE THAT A GOOD HITTER HITS .300 ONE YEAR AND DROPS TO .200 THE NEXT. EITHER YOU'RE A GOOD HITTER OR YOU ARE NOT . . .

REGGIE JACKSON

THE HOT STREAK

JUNE 14, 1969

✕

AS TOLD TO GEORGE VASS, *BASEBALL DIGEST*, JANUARY 1974

When Reggie Jackson told this story in 1974, it'd been nearly five years since he hung 10 RBIs on the Boston Red Sox in one game. It was also three years before he hit three home runs on only three pitches in the 1977 World Series.

Neither ended up being number one on his memory list, though, as he told a New York newspaper in 2017. His 1993 Hall of Fame election was tops, he said, while winning the World Series with the Oakland A's in 1973 when he was MVP and signing with the Yankees in '76 were the other leading contenders.

But when asked in '74, Jackson chose his plethora of RBIs against Boston in 1969 as the game he'd never forget. That season was just his second full year as a major leaguer, but he finished it with 47 home runs, 118 RBIs, a .608 slugging percentage and a 1.018 OPS — all of which would remain career highs.

For the record, the Red Sox pitchers that day in '69 were Ray Jarvis, Lee Stange, Bill Landis, Garry Roggenburk and Sparky Lyle, and the 10 ribbies Jackson had off them were just two short of the major league best.

—SM

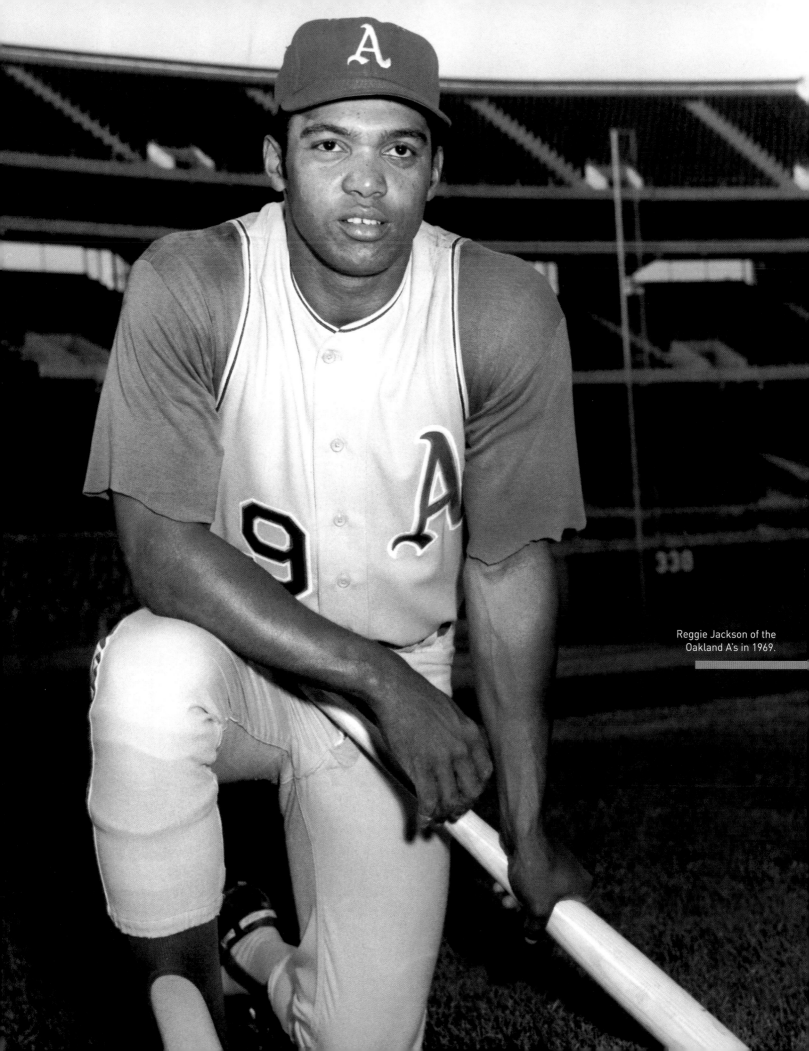

Reggie Jackson of the
Oakland A's in 1969.

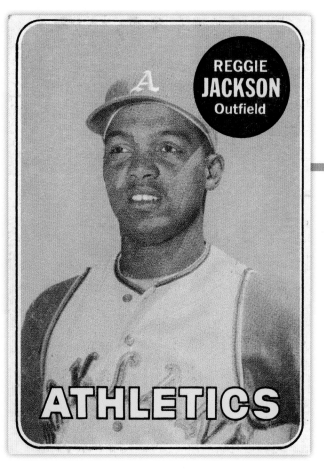

REGGIE JACKSON
Outfield

1969 Topps; #260

ATHLETICS

There's my greatest day in any sport and then there's that fifth game of the American League playoffs with the Detroit Tigers in 1972.

That second one is what most people remember because we won the pennant for Oakland when we beat the Tigers, 2–1. I got hurt and couldn't play in the World Series against Cincinnati. I had to watch on crutches as our guys beat the Reds.

I can still feel my left leg coming apart. We were losing, 1–0, in the second inning when Woodie Fryman walked me. I stole second base and got to third on an out. With Mike Epstein on first base, we pulled off a delayed double steal.

I went for the plate and I was about 30 feet away when I hurt myself. I pulled a muscle. If I stopped I'd be out, if I kept going I'd tear up my leg. We needed the run to tie so I kept going.

I could feel everything tear loose when I went into Tiger catcher Bill Freehan at the plate. I ruptured my hamstring, pulled it away from the bone and stretched the ligaments in my knee. But I was safe and we went on to win the game, 2–1, and the American League pennant.

The leg was so badly torn up that even after surgery I wasn't really sure how I'd be for the 1973 season. But, thank God, the leg came around.

So there's one game I'll never forget.

The other one? Well, it's funny, not too many people remind me of that. But when you have game like that in any sport — baseball, football, whatever — you feel like everything has come together for just that day. As a hitter when you get hot like that you just don't feel like the pitchers can ever get you out.

The game I'm talking about was on June 14, 1969 in Boston. That was the year I hit 47 home runs, 37 by the All-Star Game in July, and people were talking about me breaking Roger Maris' record of 61 home runs and comparing me to Babe Ruth.

It was my second full year with the A's, and I was just 23. But even though I was hitting all those home runs I didn't feel like another Babe Ruth. There'll never be another Ruth. I just didn't feel like a 60-home run hitter. I was just hot and in the groove and the home runs were coming.

Hank Bauer was managing the A's that year and Joe DiMaggio was one of our coaches. Both helped me a great deal.

DiMaggio helped me by always talking

BOXSCORE

	1	2	3	4	5	6	7	8	9	R	H	E
OAKLAND ATHLETICS	1	1	3	0	5	0	5	5	1	21	25	2
BOSTON RED SOX	1	0	0	0	0	3	3	0	0	7	10	6

to me about hitting. He was very encouraging and he gave me specific pointers. Bauer helped my confidence by just telling me to go up there and swing.

We went into Boston for a three-game series to start the greatest weekend I've ever had — or could hope to have. I hit a home run in the first inning Friday off Jim Lonborg with nobody on and we went on to win the game, 4–1.

It was the next day, Saturday, that I had my greatest day in sports.

I remember the first Red Sox pitcher, Ray Jarvis, but I don't know who came in after that. There were plenty of relief pitchers because we won the game, 21–7, and we got 25 hits. I was 5-for-6, but that wasn't what made it the great game it was for me.

In the first inning I drove in a run with a double. In the third inning I hit a home run with a man on and did the same in the fifth.

That was five runs batted in and when I came to bat in the sixth the bases were loaded. I figured if I could get a couple more ribbies I'd really have some kind of day. But I struck out.

That didn't bother me too much because by that time we were ahead 10–1, and I'd had about as good a day as you could expect.

But, like I say, when you're hot nothing can stop you and everything keeps breaking your way. We loaded the bases again in the seventh and I banged a single to center to drive in two more runs. Seven ribbies!

It didn't even enter my mind I'd get any more. But we kept on banging away at the Red Sox, and when I came to bat the next time, in the eighth, the bases were loaded again.

This time I hit one into the gap in right center and three runs scored. I made the turn at first but decided not to try for a double.

So there it was. I'd gone 5-for-6, with two home runs, two doubles and a single that should have been a third double. I'd driven in 10 runs in a game, which they told me later was just shy of the record.

The funny thing is that I got more hell from Bauer that day than when I struck out five times in a game. He was upset that I made a useless throw to the plate, which had let a couple runners move up. Then he dug into me for throwing on the fly and not planting my feet. Finally, he gave me hell for not making a double on the three-run single I hit in the eighth.

The way Bauer talked about my play, I was lucky I wasn't fined!

> I PULLED A MUSCLE. IF I STOPPED I'D BE OUT, IF I KEPT GOING I'D TEAR UP MY LEG. WE NEEDED THE RUN TO TIE SO I KEPT GOING.

ROD CAREW
THE HIT MACHINE

JUNE 26, 1977

AS TOLD TO GEORGE VASS, *BASEBALL DIGEST*, OCTOBER 1986

American League batting champion Rod Carew is presented his Silver Slugger award in 1976.

Rod Carew's first hit came April 11, 1967, off Baltimore's Dave McNally. His 3,000th came off Minnesota's Frank Viola on August 4, 1985, in Anaheim. Among his career 3,053 hits Carew had only 92 home runs and just 649 extra base hits overall, but he was a model of consistency. He hit over .300 for 15 straight years (1969–1983) and never hit less than .273 in any season.

The seven-time American League batting champ employed a variety of batting stances, but his most common saw him tilting backward deep in the batter's box, his bat held loosely and nearly parallel to the ground. It wasn't a home run hitter's stance, but it allowed him to spray the ball, hit line drives and bloop shots, and get to his bunting position quickly. In fact in 1977 when he hit .388 — a mark that has been topped only twice since — he dropped eight successful bunts on two-strike counts.

Midway through that '77 season, which Carew recounts here, 46,463 fans showed up at Metropolitan Stadium in Minnesota to watch Carew chase history — and Twins fans were beginning to get behind him in his pursuit.

—SM

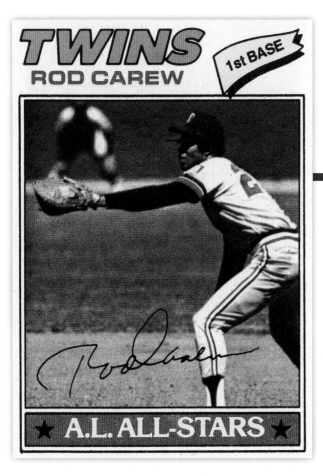

TWINS
ROD CAREW

1st BASE

★ A.L. ALL-STARS ★

1977 Topps; #120

When your major league career spans 19 seasons and you've won seven batting championships, there are all sorts of high moments. There's no way you could sort them out in order of which mean the most to you.

Naturally getting the 3,000th hit of my career ranks near the top. It was just a bloop single in the third inning, and it not only gave me a thrill but a laugh.

I'd been predicting it would be a bunt, but Bob Boone (Angels catcher) predicted it would be a typical Rod Carew hit: a bloop over third base. When I did just that I laughed remembering what Boone had said.

It made me very happy because 3,000 hits is a fine achievement. It means you've been around a long time and hit consistently. It puts you in a class with people like Ty Cobb, Rogers Hornsby, Pete Rose and Roberto Clemente. It was something I never dreamed I could accomplish when I started my career.

It may sound funny, but that 3,000th hit was not the most exciting one for me. I've always considered that to be my first hit. Your first hit in the major leagues — that's tops. It means you're on your way. When you get the first hit, then you can get the rest.

I played in four American League playoffs, two with the Minnesota Twins and two with the California Angels, but never in a World Series, so that's a bit of a disappointment.

Winning the playoffs or the World Series, now that would have been a memorable moment.

Each of the batting titles I won gave me great satisfaction, particularly the first one in 1969. To win shows you've arrived, that you're up there with the best hitters in the league.

My Most Valuable Player award is the biggest honor I've earned. I've always considered that the most prestigious award in baseball. There were some seasons I thought I should have won it, but I didn't. And I must admit I wanted it. There was a point when I thought I'd never get the MVP, especially the years I played in Minnesota. We never won a pennant there, we were far away from the big media centers of Los Angeles and New York and I wasn't a flashy, power hitter but a guy who hit to spots, who bunted and stole bases.

I even had my doubts I'd win the MVP in 1977 when I hit .400 much of the season and finished up with .388, though I thought I had a strong

JUNE 26, 1977
BOXSCORE

	1	2	3	4	5	6	7	8	9	R	H	E
CHICAGO WHITE SOX	1	0	6	1	2	0	0	0	2	12	16	2
MINNESOTA TWINS	2	6	4	3	0	0	2	2	X	19	18	0

claim. Not only were my 239 hits the highest total for a player in 47 years, but I'd also driven in 100 runs for the first time in my career. Also, that was my sixth batting title, and only Ty Cobb, Honus Wagner, Stan Musial and Rogers Hornsby had won more.

Still I had my doubts. But when I got the call that I'd been voted the AL MVP they were all set to rest. It was certainly a moment I'll never forget.

Two games in that '77 season stand out for me, not only because in some ways it was the best of my career, but for the first time I was really getting a lot of attention: I was close to hitting .400, which hadn't been done since Ted Williams in 1941.

The first game that was memorable was against the Chicago White Sox. I went into the game hitting .396 and we were in first. All that combined to fill the ballpark. I remember it was T-shirt day, and the shirts had my No. 29 on them.

I was really pumped up for that game and the crowd was on my side,

like it never had been before. Every time I came to bat they cheered for me, every time I got a hit they gave me a standing ovation. I went 4-for-5, with a homer, double and six RBIs, and we won the game. My average was up to .403.

It was the most incredible day of my life. It wasn't only the fact I was over .400, but I felt that finally the fans had accepted me and that they'd recognized me for what I was. It gave me goose bumps to feel they were behind me and that they wanted me to hit .400.

The other game I remember was the final game of the '77 season, against the Brewers in Milwaukee. I went into that game hitting .386, and my target was to match or top Williams' mark of .388 in 1957, which was the highest anyone had hit since his .406 in 1941.

I remember there were only 1,500 people in the stands for that last game of the season. It was the smallest crowd I'd seen all year, but I didn't need a crowd to push me.

The first time up I bunted to get my

first hit of the game. Then I grounded out and singled. My last time up I hit a single off the left-field wall. When the game was over, I'd gone 3-for-4 and finished the season with .388, matching Williams. That's something to remember.

I can't say I was terribly disappointed at not hitting .400. Not that it's impossible. It's just terribly hard to do. But .388 is an achievement in itself. It's something that gave me great satisfaction, and finishing up the season in that final game the way I did, going 3-for-4, made it all the more memorable.

> YOUR FIRST HIT IN THE MAJOR LEAGUES — THAT'S TOPS. IT MEANS YOU'RE ON YOUR WAY. WHEN YOU GET THE FIRST HIT, THEN YOU CAN GET THE REST.

BUCKY DENT
CURSING HIS NAME

OCTOBER 2, 1978

X

AS TOLD TO GEORGE VASS, *BASEBALL DIGEST*, SEPTEMBER 1992

He wonders here if fans would remember what he'd done, but he needn't have worried. In Boston they still never say his name without the universal adjective between "Bucky" and "Dent."

As a soft-hitting 5-foot-9, 170-pound shortstop for the New York Yankees, he usually occupied the ninth spot in the lineup and was often lifted for a pinch hitter. He was a career .247 hitter, who hit only 40 home runs over his 12 seasons in the majors, averaging one every 112.8 at-bats.

Dent had hit only .243 in the 1978 regular season for the Yankees before he essentially ended one of the most heartbreaking seasons in Red Sox history (and there have been a few of them) right in their own backyard.

Both teams had won 99 games, setting up a winner-take-all Game 163 at Fenway Park. When Dent came to bat with the Yankees down 2–0 in the seventh inning, he'd only hit four homers all season. And if not for an injured teammate and some substitutions his manager made earlier in the game, he might never have come to the plate at all.

—SM

Reggie Jackson, left, and Bucky Dent celebrate after their late-game homers help lift the Yankees over the Boston Red Sox to win the East Division and advance to the ALCS.

1978 Topps; #335

BUCKY DENT

I t wasn't until I became a manager myself that I really understood what "Lem" (manager Bob Lemon) did with me in the '78 season with the New York Yankees. At the time it really bothered me, being pinch hit for so often.

To be honest I never expected to get to bat in that situation. But luckily I did, and it gave me the greatest thrill I ever had in baseball as a player and something I hope the fans will never forget. I know I won't.

That was quite a season for us. In fact it went beyond the regular season to a tiebreaking game for the American League East championship the day after the season was supposed to end.

At one point in July we were 14 games behind the Boston Red Sox, and it looked like we might never straighten ourselves out and get back in the race. George Steinbrenner (Yankees owner) thought maybe changing managers would shake things up, so he brought in Lemon to replace Billy Martin.

Nobody will ever know whether or not we would have got going under Martin like we did with Lemon, but we began to win consistently after the change. Reggie Jackson started to get hot at the plate, and other players, like Thurman Munson and Graig Nettles — just about everybody — started playing up to their abilities. On the mound Ron Guidry was having a great season as a starter, and we had Goose Gossage coming out of the bullpen.

By early September we were rolling, and then we swept a four-game series in Boston, which Yankee teams seldom did. At one point we had something like a three-game lead over the Red Sox and were hoping we could pull away. But they had a good team, and they hung right in there. We had a one-game lead over them going into the last day of the season, but we lost and the Red Sox won, so we ended up tied for first place, setting up a tiebreaker to get into the playoffs.

I wasn't having a particularly good season up to that point — I was hitting something less than .250 — and I had a pulled right hamstring muscle that had been bothering me for quite a while. And Lemon had often pinch hit for me with men on-base or in the late innings.

Lem started Guidry, who was having the kind of season pitchers dream about (24-3), while the Red Sox had Mike Torrez, a right-hander, going for them. For a long time it looked like we couldn't do anything with Torrez.

BOXSCORE

	1	2	3	4	5	6	7	8	9	R	H	E
NEW YORK YANKEES	0	0	0	0	0	0	4	1	0	5	8	0
BOSTON RED SOX	0	1	0	0	0	1	0	2	0	4	11	0

Meanwhile Boston had gotten a couple runs early off Guidry — I think "Yaz" (Carl Yastrzemski) hit a home run.

In the seventh inning we finally got a chance. With one out Chris Chambliss and Roy White got singles. But Jim Spencer flied out and I was to be the next batter.

I was in the on-deck circle, but I was waiting for Lem to call me back for a pinch hitter. In that situation I never expected to bat. But we were without Willie Randolph because of a hamstring injury, and we were out of infielders because Spencer had pinch hit for Brian Doyle. Lem had no choice but to let me hit.

I wasn't thinking home run. All I was thinking about was hitting the ball hard.

That at-bat I'll remember all my life. I took the first pitch for a ball then fouled the next one off my left ankle. It was really painful and I hobbled around. While I was doing that Mickey Rivers yelled at me to change bats. I'd been using his bats and he told me the one I had was chipped and I should switch to a good one, which I did.

When I returned to bat, Torrez threw me a fastball, belt high and inside. He'd thrown that pitch to me before and handcuffed me. But I was hoping to see it again. I knew how Torrez pitched — he'd been with us the year before — and I knew I could drive a pitch like that.

In Fenway Park that wall in left field is always on your mind, and when he threw me that pitch again, I jumped on it. I knew right away I'd hit it well. It was high and deep and landed on top of the screen about 10 feet fair for a home run to put us ahead 3–2.

When I hit it, seeing that ball go up on the screen was the greatest thing in the world. It was like a fairy tale come true.

We scored another run before the inning was over, and Jackson hit a home run in the eighth to make it 5–2. The Red Sox scored a couple runs in the bottom of the inning and had two men on-base in the ninth before Gos-

sage got Yaz to pop out, ending the game, 5–4, and giving us the division title.

When I was a kid I used to dream about hitting a home run in a situation like that. It was like Bobby Thomson's home run in 1951. I was too young to see that, but like everybody else I've heard the replays of the broadcast with the announcer (Russ Hodges) screaming, "The Giants win the pennant! The Giants win the pennant!"

To me this home run was like that. I'll never forget it.

I won't forget the championship series or the World Series, either. We beat the Kansas City Royals to win the pennant. Then the World Series was something like the regular season — we came from behind against the Los Angeles Dodgers, being down 2-0 in the Series after the first two games, and won it. I had a good series (.417 with seven RBIs) and was named MVP, which is something I can be proud of.

But nothing can top that home run — nothing.

GEORGE BRETT
A ROYAL PAIN IN THE BUTT

JULY 24, 1983

AS TOLD TO GEORGE VASS, *BASEBALL DIGEST*, JANUARY 1995

George Brett was the only player to win batting titles in three different decades. But he is also remembered for two rare, and somewhat odd, baseball situations.

In the one he refers to here, from the 1983 season, he hit a two-run homer at Yankee Stadium in the top of the ninth inning off Goose Gossage to lift the Kansas City Royals to a 5–4 win. But Yankees manager Billy Martin protested that the pine tar on Brett's bat extended beyond the allowable 18 inches from the bottom of his bat. It was a little-known rule that seemed to have no purpose. After measuring it against home plate, umpire Tim McClelland called Brett out. The homer was negated and the Royals lost. The tape of Brett wildly storming after McClelland has been a staple of all-time highlight reels. American League president Lee MacPhail eventually ruled that the tar hadn't helped Brett hit the home run and ordered the game replayed at a later date with the Royals up 5–4 with two out in the top of the ninth.

Three years earlier Brett had gained unwanted attention for his battle with hemorrhoids during the 1980 World Series.

—SM

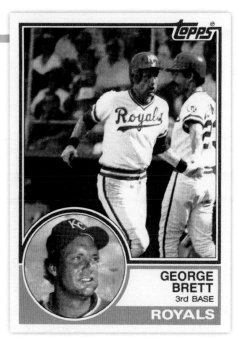

GEORGE
BRETT
3rd BASE
ROYALS

or three years after that 1980 World Series everywhere I went I was that guy — the guy with a pain in his butt. I was "The Hemorrhoids Guy" in every stadium.

But that all changed on July 24, 1983.

I didn't find this out until years later, but in a series against the Yankees in Kansas City two weeks before the incident, Graig Nettles thought he saw the pine tar too far up my bat. He told Goose Gossage that if I got a big hit they were going to show the umpires the bat and try to get it overturned. It didn't become an issue then, so they let it go. Little did I know what they had planned for me when we got to New York a couple weeks later.

Of course Billy Martin was in on it. He was always looking for an angle.

Here's something you probably didn't know about that day. When a player hits a home run, the batboy is supposed to get the bat and take it back to the bat rack, where it mixes in with all the other bats. If our batboy had done that, they wouldn't have had the bat. But the kid was a George Brett fan in New York. I loved him. He wanted to shake my hand after I crossed the plate. So there he was, waiting for me at home and holding the bat when I came in. He was just standing there holding it like a smoking gun. That's what gave Billy and those guys the opportunity, though, I wasn't trying to hide anything. The bat was legal.

Frank White was sitting next to me on the bench, and he said he didn't like what he was seeing out there, four umpires surrounded by Billy and all the Yankees. He said, "This doesn't look good. They're going to call you out." I said, "Call me out? For what? If they do I'm going to go out there and raise hell." And just as I finished saying that, the ump walked over and gave me the out sign.

I went nuts. I was going to get my money's worth.

While I was arguing, Gaylord Perry grabbed the bat from the umpire and ran toward our dugout. Gaylord was big into memorabilia, so he must have wanted it for his collection. He tossed it to someone, who tossed it to someone else, and it wound up in Steve Renko's hands at the end of the tunnel before the clubhouse. There was no one else to toss it to. The security guards and the umpires chased them all up the tunnel and got the bat.

When we went to New York 25 days later to finish the game, I watched the last four outs from an Italian restaurant in Newark because I had been thrown out of the game for charging the umpires — even though the game was over. Larry Ameche, who was (singer) Don Ameche's son and our flight rep at the time, joined me for a nice meal while the guys went and finished the game. We watched on TV as Dan Quisenberry retired the Yankees for the win.

I don't really have any bad memories about what happened. I went from The Hemorrhoids Guy to "The Pine Tar Guy," which was much better for me. So, I always made sure to give my thanks to Billy Martin because I went from something pretty embarrassing to being remembered for hitting a home run. It worked out very well for me.

JULY 24, 1983
BOXSCORE

	1	2	3	4	5	6	7	8	9	R	H	E
KANSAS CITY ROYALS	0	1	0	1	0	1	0	0	2	5	13	0
NEW YORK YANKEES	0	1	0	0	0	3	0	0	0	4	8	0

RYNE SANDBERG
GAME OF HIS LIFE

JUNE 23, 1984

AS TOLD TO BARRY ROZNER, *BASEBALL DIGEST*, NOVEMBER 2012

When Jim Frey took over as manager in 1984 the Cubs had finished 20 games below .500 and hadn't reached the postseason in 39 years. That spring Chicago traded for Bob Dernier, Gary Matthews, Dennis Eckersley and Rick Sutcliffe, and during spring training Frey got Ryne Sandberg, a pull hitter who didn't hit homers, to open up and swing for power. Sandberg would end the season as NL MVP as the Cubs won the National League East.

"The Sandberg Game" (as it's known in Chicago) was a nationally televised Saturday afternoon Game of the Week on NBC, which was a big deal at the time. Chicago was losing to St. Louis 9–8 going into the bottom of the ninth and then 11–9 in the bottom of the 10th. But the Cubs would eventually win 12–11 in the 11th inning, though not before Sandberg burst into national prominence. He was already 3-for-4 with four RBIs by the ninth inning when he faced legendary closer Bruce Sutter and his lethal splitter. And in the 10th inning the Cubs were down to their final out, with one on, when Sandberg came to the plate against Sutter again.

—SM

Ryne Sandberg slugs a triple against Cincinnati at Wrigley Field in 1984.

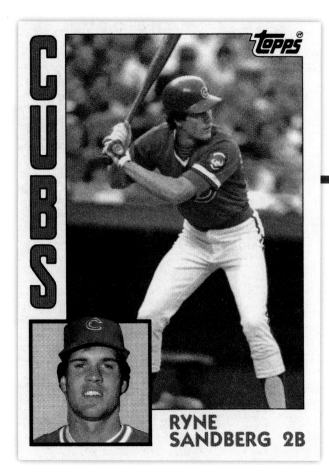

CUBS

Topps

1984 Topps; #596

RYNE
SANDBERG 2B

When I left the dugout in the bottom of the ninth "Sarge" (Matthews) was talking to me about the splitter, and how it would break down and in hard to a right-handed hitter. I felt no pressure because no one expected me to get a hit in that situation, and my first couple years I had trouble with those hard, down-and-in pitches.

Jim Frey had helped me change my thinking on that type of pitch. With his coaching I was able to get to that spot; I'd open up quickly and be aggressive with those pitches. That was working for me in 1984, and I had that in mind when I went to the plate against Sutter. I kept repeating to myself everything Frey had told me in spring training: "Open up

and swing inside. Open up and swing inside."

Sutter always pitched out of the stretch. As I looked at him get set and right himself for his delivery I thought the pitch would be there and I was only thinking those words: Open up and swing inside. Open up and swing inside. I kept saying those words in my head as the pitch came toward home plate. It was exactly in that spot, right where Frey had taught me to look and where Sarge said it would be. I opened up and swung inside and I crushed it. It was gone.

Sutter knew it. Announcer Bob Costas knew it. The fans knew it. But at first I thought it might be off the wall so I was running hard. The line

drive landed in the bleachers, and before I hit first base Wrigley Field erupted. It was the loudest I had ever heard it in my three years there. I couldn't feel my hands or my feet as I tried to get around the bases. I was numb. I was floating on air.

I was in a fog. It's like an out-of-body experience, I guess. I was there observing it, but I wasn't really there. It was too big, apparently, for me to handle the moment. (Third-base coach) Don Zimmer snapped me back to reality when he shook my hand and smacked me on the back. When I crossed home plate I'm pretty sure the ground was shaking. Maybe that was just my legs being wobbly.

When I got to the dugout I never had that feeling during a baseball game before. It was like I threw a game-winning touchdown. The guys were hugging me and jumping on me. It was a wild scene.

When I came up in the 10th I

BOXSCORE

	1	2	3	4	5	6	7	8	9	10	11	R	H	E
ST. LOUIS CARDINALS	1	6	0	0	0	2	0	0	0	2	0	11	13	1
CHICAGO CUBS	1	0	0	0	2	5	0	0	1	2	1	12	14	2

didn't know what to think. As I walked to the plate the crowd was starting to stand and cheer, and I was trying to think about what Sutter would do this time. He wouldn't go to the same splitter on the first pitch again, right? Probably not. Definitely not in that same spot.

On the other hand 99 times out of 100 that pitch was unhittable. I figured I had nothing to lose. I had a home run already, so I figured he was thinking I wouldn't believe he'd throw the same pitch in the same spot. So I guessed he'd do just that.

I had those same swing thoughts again. Open up and swing inside. I figured maybe I could double into the corner, score a run, get in scoring position and give us a chance to tie.

It was the same pitch, same location, same swing, except this time I knew it was gone off the bat. It was a line drive that cleared the left-center field wall by about 10 feet and landed pretty close to where the first one did. It felt too good to be true.

I peeked at Sutter and I remember how he reacted when the ump threw him a ball. He stabbed at it with his mitt in total disgust.

I floated around the bases again, kind of in shock. This time when I got to home plate half the team was waiting for me. It was total bedlam. Guys were jumping on me. I was worried the umps would be mad that we were all over the field. I was worried Sutter would be mad. We were acting like we won the pennant. It was completely insane.

We rode the high from that game all the way into the playoffs. The Cubs weren't lovable losers anymore, either. For the first time in a long time we were a real baseball team, and we sent notice to the National League that we were for real.

To this day fans ask me about "The Sandberg Game" and talk about where they were when they saw it. That game

forced me to try to match that level of play every single day for the rest of my career, thinking I would let people down if I didn't do that. I learned that I could be that good and that I had to try to be that good every day. Frey's teaching and those two pitches from Sutter changed my career. It was the turning point for my career. Really, when you look back on it now, it completely changed my life.

> I COULDN'T FEEL MY HANDS OR MY FEET AS I TRIED TO GET AROUND THE BASES. I WAS NUMB. I WAS FLOATING ON AIR.

ANDRE DAWSON
BIG DAY AT WRIGLEY

SEPTEMBER 24, 1985

AS TOLD TO GEORGE VASS, *BASEBALL DIGEST*, JANUARY 1987

Andre Dawson is one of only three players (Willie McCovey and Jeff King) to hit two homers in the same inning twice in their careers. Both times came on the road as a Montreal Expo: one in Atlanta in 1978 and the other in 1985 at his home away from home, Wrigley Field.

A month after Dawson told this account of that second game, in Chicago, he became a Cub through free agency. Up until then he'd played his entire career in Montreal, where he hit in the cavernous Olympic Stadium. The switch to playing half his games at Wrigley helped propel "The Hawk" to the National League MVP award in 1987 after he finished with 49 home runs, 137 RBIs and a .568 slugging percentage — all would be career highs.

Dawson played only five more seasons in Chicago, but his time there left an indelible mark on him. When he was inducted into the Hall of Fame in 2010 he asked to go in as a Cub. The request was ultimately turned down, since his 11 years as an Expo took precedent, but it showed the soft spot Dawson had for the franchise and the city.

—SM

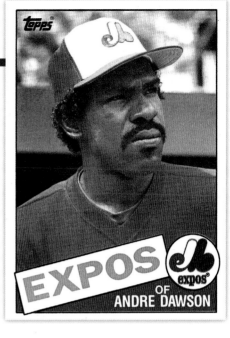

I've always liked to hit at Wrigley, but I never expected to have a game like the one I had in 1985 when I hit three home runs in one of the wildest games I've ever been involved in.

The strange thing is that the last four or five years home runs haven't come for me like they used to earlier in my career. I still hit as many over a season, but in spurts rather than consistently. I used to hit four, five home runs every month, about one every week. Now I'll go two, three weeks without one, then hit four or five in a few days.

I've tried to analyze why that has been the case for me, but I can't figure it out. I know that when you get into a streak you see the ball better, and that the pitcher will throw you the pitch you want to hit earlier in the count. When you're not going as well you never see your pitch, you walk or never get good wood on the ball. I think that's the case for most every hitter.

My three-home run day in Chicago in '85 typifies the way things go for a batter. At one point you can't do anything right, then all of a sudden you hit everything in sight.

At the time I was in a stretch of 1-for-23 heading into a series in St. Louis before we went to Chicago, and I hadn't hit a home run in nearly three weeks. In the second game against the Cardinals I hit a grand slam. I hit another home run in that series before we went to Chicago where in the first game I hit another.

The next game, the one I'll never forget, was about as crazy. We'd hit five home runs the previous day so we knew anything could happen, but nobody could have predicted what actually would.

When I came to bat in the first inning we had a man on and Ray Fontenot, a left-hander, was pitching for the Cubs. He gave me a pitch to hit and I did: a two-run homer.

We took a 3–2 lead into the fifth inning, and then everything broke loose. We scored 12 runs and I came to bat twice with two men on. Each time I hit a home run — the first one off Fontenot, the other one off of Jon Perlman, a rookie right-hander.

When the dust cleared in the fifth we had a 15–2 lead, and I'd hit three home runs and driven in eight runs on the day.

That wasn't the end of it, though. I got another hit and finished up 4-for-6 that day.

What really stands out is that we almost lost the game. The Cubs kept hammering away until they closed to within two runs. We eventually won 17–15.

We needed every run I drove in that day, and then some. You don't forget a game like that.

SEPTEMBER 24, 1985
BOXSCORE

	1	2	3	4	5	6	7	8	9	R	H	E
MONTREAL EXPOS	2	1	0	0	12	0	0	2	0	17	17	1
CHICAGO CUBS	0	0	0	2	0	1	3	4	5	15	20	2

Dave Henderson, left, and Rich Gedman celebrate Henderson's ninth-inning homer in Game 5 of the 1986 ALCS.

DAVE HENDERSON
FROM ZERO TO HERO

OCTOBER 12, 1986

AS TOLD TO GEORGE VASS, *BASEBALL DIGEST*, JULY 1988

Dave Henderson's favorite memory is probably the least favorite of every California Angels fan.

Henderson was traded in mid-August to Boston from Seattle, where earlier in the year as a Mariner he accounted for three of a record 20 strikeouts by soon-to-be teammate Roger Clemens. Two months later he helped put the Red Sox into the World Series after the Angels had them one strike from extinction.

It was Henderson's first trip to the Fall Classic. He'd been used primarily off the bench with the Red Sox to that point, but after his heroics in California, manager John McNamara started Henderson in all seven games. And just as it looked like the Red Sox had lost the division series versus the Angels, it looked like they had won the World Series against the Mets — until Mookie Wilson's grounder went through Bill Buckner's legs in Game 6.

Henderson went to three more World Series, all with Oakland, where he won the 1989 championship with the A's. But Game 5 against the Angels still stands out the most for him. And to think, earlier in the game a gaffe in the outfield almost made him the fall guy.

—SM

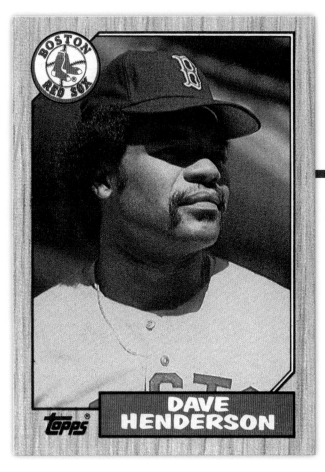

1987 Topps; #452

DAVE HENDERSON

Topps®

T here's no doubt one of the best things that ever happened to me in baseball was being traded to Boston late in the 1986 season. That trade from Seattle made it possible for me to enjoy some of the greatest thrills a player can have. I got to play in a league championship series and then in the World Series with the Red Sox just a few weeks after I joined them.

If I'd stayed with the Mariners, who knows if I'd ever have gotten the chance. I've known and heard of a lot of players with long careers who have never had the opportunity to play in a World Series. That's something every player hopes to do. I'm lucky I've had the experience.

When the Red Sox traded for me I knew it was to fill in occasionally in the outfield, to come off the bench and to be ready to do a job at all times. Like any other player I would have preferred to play every day, but all you can do sometimes is stay ready and do the best job you can when they call on you.

During the season I started a few games in center field for the Red Sox and filled in defensively for Tony Armas in center from time to time as we won the American League East Division championship. I can't say I expected to play much in the playoffs against California. I just hoped I'd do well when I did. Sometimes it's better like that because you don't have great expectations, you don't put pressure on yourself. Maybe that's why I did

well when I did get to play. I felt relaxed. Maybe what I was doing didn't sink in until afterward.

I got to play in the late innings of a couple of the first four games against the Angels, but it was the fifth game that things really started to make an impression. A lot of people at the time said it was one of the greatest, if not the greatest game ever played. I don't know about that, but I do know it ranks on top for me.

We were down three games to one in the championship series to the Angels, and for a while in the fifth game it looked like they were going to put us away and win the American League pennant. We were leading, 2–1, in the fifth inning when John McNamara put me in center field because Armas was hurt. An inning later came the play that almost made me the goat.

The Angels had a man on second base in the sixth inning when Bobby Grich hit a drive to center. I knew I'd have to go to the wall and leap

BOXSCORE

	1	2	3	4	5	6	7	8	9	10	11	R	H	E
BOSTON RED SOX	0	2	0	0	0	0	0	0	4	0	1	7	12	0
CALIFORNIA ANGELS	0	0	1	0	0	2	2	0	1	0	0	6	13	0

to catch it. The ball hit the heel of my glove as I was going up, but I had it in the pocket until my wrist hit the top of the wall. The ball fell over the fence for a two-run homer that gave California a 3–2 lead.

I felt bad about it. But ballplayers are accustomed to failure because, to be honest, we fail a lot of the time. I hoped I'd get a chance to make up for it.

It didn't look like that chance would come. By the top of the ninth inning the Angels were leading, 5–2, and just three outs away from winning the pennant. But we got a man on and Don Baylor hit a two-run homer to make it 5–4.

When I came to bat there was a man on-base, two out and Donnie Moore was pitching for the Angels. I tried to relax, but I knew that if I didn't get on-base it was all over. The count moved up to 2-2 when Moore threw me a fastball, the pitch I was looking for, but I didn't quite get a hold of it and fouled it off.

The next pitch was a forkball and I hammered it. When I hit it I knew it was gone. I've hit enough homers in my career to know the feeling.

That put us ahead, 6–5, but California came back with a run in the bottom of the ninth to send us into extra innings.

We went into the 11th inning, and when I came to bat we had the bases loaded. This time I hit a sacrifice fly to give us the lead, 7–6. We held onto that to win the game and then won the next two in Boston for the pennant.

That's the game I'll never forget, for sure, though just playing in the World Series, even though we lost to the Mets, ranks right up there with my top moments in the game.

McNamara kept me in the lineup for all the games against the Mets, and I had a real good Series. I batted .400 and hit a couple home runs.

If we'd won the Series I'm sure Game 6 would have been my greatest moment. We went into the 10th inning tied, 3–3, and I hit a homer off Rick

Aguilera to make it 4–3. When we scored another run to go up by two, it looked as though we were about to win the Series.

I thought it was the closing chapter of a fairy tale. But the Mets came back with three runs to win that game, 6–5, and send the Series to a seventh game, which they won as well.

That was a tremendous disappointment. But all the same I had my moments in those playoffs and that World Series, and I'll never forget them.

> . . . BALLPLAYERS ARE ACCUSTOMED TO FAILURE BECAUSE, TO BE HONEST, WE FAIL A LOT OF THE TIME.

TIM RAINES
STICKING IT TO THE OWNERS

MAY 2, 1987

✕

AS TOLD TO BARRY ROZNER, *BASEBALL DIGEST*, NOVEMBER 2016

At the end of the 1986 season Major League Baseball owners colluded to prevent free agents from landing ever-escalating contracts. It was one of the ugliest periods in labor relations in the history of the game.

Tim Raines was among many top players who were unable to cash in on their career successes. He had been a dominant leadoff hitter the previous four years, averaging 111 runs, 76 stolen bases, a .315 batting average and .454 slugging percentage. He should have been courted by several teams but found no bona fide takers and had to accept a three-year $4.8 million offer from Montreal he'd already rejected. To make matters worse, by MLB rules he couldn't re-sign until May 1.

The next day he returned to face the Mets in New York. He tripled in his first at-bat, singled to help tie the game in the ninth inning and then hit a grand slam in the 10th to stake the Expos to the win.

In six plate appearances Raines finished with four hits, a walk, four RBIs, nine total bases and a stolen base. It was a symbolic middle finger to the teams who passed on him because of collusion.

—SM

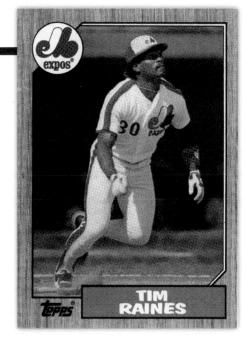

TIM RAINES

he entire thing was miserable and frustrating. What was supposed to be great for me turned out to be terrible. That's what collusion did to me that year.

It was a joke. I had a few teams talk to me, but they weren't real offers. I went to the Houston camp and they said they'd give me less than a million. I was already making more than that the year before, so did they think I would take it?

It was a really rough time. I had spent my career earning a chance to be a free agent and go somewhere where I had a chance to win right away. You want both, right? You want to sign for the best deal and you want to compete for a World Series.

The hard part is there just wasn't anything happening out there. It was a month before the season and I didn't have a job, so I decided to go back to Montreal because I really didn't have any options.

Then I found out I couldn't play the first month of the season. I couldn't even attend spring training, so I worked out on my own in Florida.

I was actually in better shape than I had been in for a few years. I was running every day, lifting weights and I was hitting with a high school team in Sarasota. So I felt pretty good going into that first game.

Still I thought there would be some rust. I was pretty nervous, too, and I was also mad. I knew I had something to prove.

Batting practice didn't go well. I don't think I got one ball out of the cage. There were cameras everywhere and I was feeling the heat. I hadn't been with the team for eight months, so it was a pretty weird feeling to be back. It was like getting called up from the minors to the big leagues. I had a lot of nerves that day.

The first pitch I saw from David Cone I hit it off the right-field wall. All of a sudden, running to first, everything felt right again in my world. I was just playing baseball again. I remember standing on third and thinking that I was back in the big leagues and it was all good.

It was a wild game that kept going back and forth, and it was a long one. I had two more singles before I came to the plate in the 10th and hit the grand slam. It was an incredible moment, and I couldn't quite believe that it was happening. It was like I was having a nightmare and then it was over all of a sudden. It happened that fast.

However, looking back, what I was proudest of wasn't so much the grand slam, but a single I hit as the lead batter in the ninth. It was a bouncer that I didn't hit well. I had to hustle to make it to first ahead of the throw. If I didn't get that hit we might not have tied the game, and I wouldn't have had the opportunity for that grand slam.

That game was one of those crazy things that can happen in baseball, but I think I wanted to show all those owners in collusion that they made a big mistake. I definitely had something to prove. I'll never forget that day, that's for sure.

MAY 2, 1987
BOXSCORE

	1	2	3	4	5	6	7	8	9	10	R	H	E
MONTREAL EXPOS	0	1	2	0	0	1	0	0	2	5	11	20	1
NEW YORK METS	0	0	1	3	0	2	0	0	0	1	7	13	3

JOE GIRARDI
TRIPLE THE FUN

OCTOBER 26, 1996

AS TOLD TO BARRY ROZNER, *BASEBALL DIGEST*, JANUARY 2014

When the New York Yankees needed a catcher to join backup Jim Leyritz, they went out and got Joe Girardi from the Colorado Rockies after the 1995 season. He would win three World Series in his four years as a player with the Yankees and another in his 10-year tenure as their manager, which lasted through 2017.

Girardi had five hits as the Yankees dispatched the Texas Rangers and Baltimore Orioles to get to the 1996 World Series. There they faced the defending champion Atlanta Braves, who had John Smoltz, about to win the Cy Young Award that season, and Greg Maddux, who'd won the previous four. The Yankees dropped the first two games at home, then won the next three in Atlanta.

Maddux, Girardi's former teammate with the Chicago Cubs, was on the mound for the Braves in Game 6 in New York. The catcher's RBI triple in the third inning started a three-run burst that led to the 3–2 victory and the World Series title. It would be Girardi's only RBI in 39 career postseason games. Before it he had gone 0-for-7 in three games against the Braves.

—SM

1996 Topps; #36

im always caught Andy Pettitte that year. That's the kind of team we had. We all bought in, even though some pretty big names got platooned sometimes.

Look at that fifth game. We won 1–0. "Straw" (Darryl Strawberry) started in left field and Tim Raines sat. Charlie Hayes played third and Wade Boggs sat. Cecil Fielder was at first and Tino Martinez sat. We all shared at-bats, and it worked extremely well because everyone wanted to win. That was number one on our minds. It was just a tremendous group of guys.

In Game 6 when I came up against Maddux in the third inning with Paul O'Neill on third, I wondered if I might get the squeeze sign. During the course of the season I probably tried 10 or 12 safety squeezes. But their infield defense was so good and Maddux won a Gold Glove 18 times during his career, so I wasn't told to bunt.

I knew Greg. From facing him and catching him in Chicago I knew he relied on command and movement of the fastball as much as any pitch he had. I knew he would give me a fastball at some point in that at-bat, and I was going be ready for the first one.

I couldn't afford to fall behind 0-1 and have him nibble me to death on the corners. I was swinging first pitch and just hoping he got the sinker up a little to give me a fighting chance.

As it happened, the first pitch was up a bit, and I hit it just over Marquis Grissom's head in center field for a triple. Atlanta's outfielders played very shallow. Their pitchers were so good and they broke so many bats and made guys take bad swings that they wanted the outfielders making sure there were never any cheap hits falling in front of them. That's probably why that ball got over his head.

It happened so fast that I didn't take it in as much as I should have. O'Neill said it was the loudest he ever heard Yankee Stadium. But I didn't even hear it. I was thinking: how do I get our pitcher, Jimmy Key, through five innings and turn it over to the bullpen?

After Mark Lemke fouled out to Charlie Hayes to end the game, I don't remember the first few minutes at all. I was like a little kid screaming after getting the greatest present ever on Christmas.

You think you understand what it will feel like to win the World Series, but you really have no idea until it happens, and then it all comes pouring out. It's all the sacrifice you've made to get there, all the sacrifice your wife has made, all the sacrifice your mom and dad made all their lives to help you get there, all the sacrifices your coaches and teammates made. It's just pure joy, and my wife was there to see it and my dad was there to see it.

It was the biggest hit of my career. I'm not a person who says, "I wish I could go back and play. I wish I was 18 years old again." I don't ever think like that. I like my life. But if there is one moment in time I wish I could go back and live again, it would be standing on third base.

Not to bask in it, but to soak it in and understand the moment — to feel it.

OCTOBER 26, 1996
BOXSCORE

	1	2	3	4	5	6	7	8	9	R	H	E
ATLANTA BRAVES	0	0	0	1	0	0	0	0	1	2	8	0
NEW YORK YANKEES	0	0	3	0	0	0	0	0	X	3	8	1

SANDY KOUFAX

NO ROOM FOR ERROR

SEPTEMBER 9, 1965

✕

AS TOLD TO GEORGE VASS, *BASEBALL DIGEST*, MAY 1977

Although he played a dozen seasons for the Dodgers in Brooklyn and Los Angeles, it was the final half of his abbreviated career that made Sandy Koufax one of the greatest pitchers of all time.

Arthritis in his pitching (left) elbow forced him to retire after the 1966 season, at the age of 30, just over a year after the perfect game he mentions here. But from 1961 to 1966 he was absolutely dominant. The first pitcher to win three Cy Young Awards, Koufax won them all unanimously when there was only one award for the two leagues combined. He won the pitching Triple Crown (wins, ERA and strike-outs) each of those seasons and also was the first pitcher to throw four no-hitters.

In the five weeks after the perfect game, Koufax went 4-1 to finish the regular season. His only loss was 2–1 in his next start to the team (and pitcher) he beat in his perfect game. He then went 2-1 in the Dodgers' World Series victory over the Minnesota Twins. He didn't pitch Game 1 because of Yom Kippur, but he won Games 5 and 7 with complete-game shutouts.

—SM

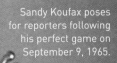
Sandy Koufax poses
for reporters following
his perfect game on
September 9, 1965.

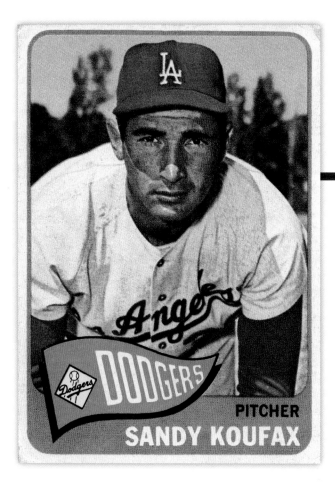

1965 Topps; #300

PITCHER

SANDY KOUFAX

I wouldn't say it was the most memorable game of my career, though it certainly was one of them.

It possibly was Bob Hendley's most memorable game, because I doubt if he ever pitched a better one for the Chicago Cubs. With any sort of luck Hendley would have won that game, but as so often happens to a pitcher he was working on a day when his team couldn't score a run.

It's often been said that pitching a no-hitter involves a lot of luck because everything has to go right for you. Anything can happen to break it up. A pop fly can land between three fielders, none of whom can quite reach it. A grounder can take a hop or find a hole in the infield.

As for a perfect game, that's even more of an accident, if you can compare degrees of such things. It's unthinkable. It just happens.

It happened to me in 1965. I pitched a perfect game against the Cubs for the fourth no-hitter of my career, something no pitcher had ever done before.

Hendley gave up one hit, and that was a blooper. Ironically it had nothing to do with the run that was scored.

I had more than 20 wins at that point of the season, but I'd lost my last three decisions. We just weren't getting too many runs when the Cubs came into L.A. for one game, which was a strange bit of scheduling.

The Cubs were down in the standings, but they had a good hitting team.

They had real power with Ron Santo, Ernie Banks, Billy Williams, Harvey Kuenn and some others.

At the start of the game I didn't have anything special, just average stuff. The fastball didn't have the zip it sometimes did, and the curveball didn't break sharply. But as the game went on my fastball really came alive. It began to pop as well as it had all season.

The Cubs were going down 1-2-3 inning after inning, but we weren't having much better luck against Hendley. He was getting the side out, too, with his sinker working and our batters beating it into the ground.

In the fifth inning we got a run, but it was without a hit, and it was typical of the way we'd been scoring all year. We got a break and took advantage of it. Lou Johnson walked and Ron Fairly moved him to second with a sacrifice bunt. The way the game was going a run looked pretty big at that point, so Johnson decided to try and steal third, from where he might be able to score

BOXSCORE

	1	2	3	4	5	6	7	8	9	R	H	E
CHICAGO CUBS	0	0	0	0	0	0	0	0	0	0	0	1
LOS ANGELES DODGERS	0	0	0	0	1	0	0	0	X	1	1	0

on a sacrifice fly or a ball hit to the right side of the infield.

When Johnson slid into third, catcher Chris Krug's throw sailed into left field, down the line. Johnson picked himself up and scored on the error.

I can't say I felt terrible about Hendley getting a bad break like that while pitching so well. I was hoping we'd get six more runs and put the game away.

We weren't about to, though. As it turned out we were lucky even to get a hit. It didn't come until the seventh inning. Johnson blooped a pop fly down the right-field line and it landed for a double. That was the only thing that kept Hendley from pitching a losing no-hitter while I was pitching the perfect game.

I don't remember any exceptional fielding plays early in the game, and there really weren't many opportunities for them. I struck out a lot of Cubs, especially after my fastball came around. I had good control, too. I was consistently ahead of the hitters, until

Williams came to bat in the seventh inning with two out.

I fell behind 3-0. I didn't try to finesse him. I couldn't afford to. If I walked Williams, Santo was next up. He could hit the ball out of the park, and that 1–0 lead would be gone. So I challenged Williams. I threw the ball as hard as I could down the pike and got him to end the inning.

That was seven complete innings, but nobody on either bench said anything about a no-hitter. Usually the team in the other dugout will let you know, hoping to shake you up, to break your concentration. But nobody in the Chicago dugout said anything, or if they did I didn't hear it.

The eighth inning I was throwing as hard as I ever had, not thinking so much about the perfect game as about the 1–0 lead, which could disappear with one swing of the bat. I wasn't necessarily trying to strike everybody out, but just to keep the ball low and away so they'd hit it in the dirt. I didn't

want to get anything up, because they had the hitters that would kill a pitch like that.

I struck out Santo to start the eighth and then the next two batters. I still had the perfect game going and there was no way I could relax, not with a 1–0 lead.

The first two batters in the ninth struck out, and then it came down to the last man — Kuenn, who was pinch-hitting for Hendley.

Kuenn was a great hitter, even though he was near the end of his career. I had a lot of respect for him. He hit the ball where it was pitched and was hard to fool. He almost always got a piece of the ball.

I gave him everything I had. Three fastballs, right down the pike. The third one, my 14th strikeout, ended the game.

A perfect game for me and disappointment for Hendley. He'd given up just one hit, a blooper at that.

I sympathized with him, up to a point, and only after we'd won.

Bob Gibson shows his signature, balletic delivery during a game in 1968.

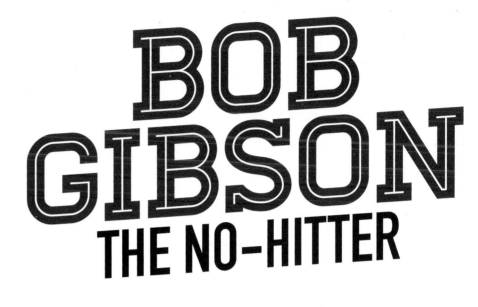

BOB GIBSON
THE NO-HITTER

AUGUST 14, 1971

AS TOLD TO GEORGE VASS, *BASEBALL DIGEST*, DECEMBER 1974

Bob Gibson was the best pitcher in baseball in 1968's Year of the Pitcher, which compelled Major League Baseball to lower the mound from 15 inches to 10 for the start of the 1969 season. The collective 2.98 ERA among major league pitchers in 1968 had been the lowest in 50 years, and Gibson had a stunning 1.12 ERA with 268 strikeouts and just 62 walks. Of his 34 starts, he failed to complete only six of them, and he registered 13 shutouts.

Gibson had a searing fastball, complemented by a vicious slider, and he had a mean streak on the mound. He would knock down or brush back opposing batters with high heat, especially if they'd been successful against him.

A nine-time All-Star Gibson won two Cy Young Awards and one National League MVP. He spent his entire 17-year career in St. Louis where he won a pair of World Series (1964 and 1967) with the Cardinals and was Series MVP both times. But as he recalls here his most memorable game came in the heat of a pennant race, three seasons after the mounds had been lowered.

—SM

CARDS
bob gibson • pitcher

1971 Topps; #450

Robert Gibson

I know somebody's going to say what about the World Series game against the Detroit Tigers in 1968 when you struck out 17 men? Isn't that the one, the game you'll never forget? Sure, that game was a big one, not because I struck out 17 men but because I won it. You're always proud when you've done an exceptionally good job because that's what you're out there for. That's what they pay you to do.

But when I think about it, though, it's not difficult to single out the game I remember best. No doubt about it, it's the no-hitter I pitched against the Pittsburgh Pirates.

Why do I choose that game above all the others, the ones in World Series play or in pennant races or when I've struck out a lot of men? The reason is that a no-hitter is something you just don't set out to do. It just happens. You can say to yourself, "I've got to win this game today" or "I've got to pitch the best I can," but you never go out there and say you are going to pitch a no-hitter. It can't be done.

A no-hitter is pitched because of a perfect combination of circumstances. The pitcher usually has good stuff, but he's also got luck on his side. Line drives are hit right at somebody, pop flies don't drop in and the wind blows in and keeps a long fly ball from being a home run. Everything works out perfectly.

You could almost say a no-hitter is an accident — a pleasant accident but a completely unexpected and unplanned event all the same.

That 1971 season was sort of up and down for me. I tore a thigh muscle in May and was on the disabled list for 21 days. I got off to a slow start, but on August 4th I got my 200th career victory to give me 10 wins for the season.

In mid-August we went into Pittsburgh to play a four-game series. We were coming up fast, but were still eight games behind the Pirates. As it turned out we swept the four games to cut the Pirates' lead to four, though they went on to win the division.

But I wasn't thinking about anything other than winning the game I started against the Pirates on Saturday night, August 14. A no-hitter was the furthest thing from my mind.

Besides I never figured to pitch one. You know, I always got the ball up high. Somebody was bound to make good contact with it at least once in a while.

BOXSCORE

	1	2	3	4	5	6	7	8	9	R	H	E
ST. LOUIS CARDINALS	5	0	0	0	3	0	0	3	0	11	16	0
PITTSBURGH PIRATES	0	0	0	0	0	0	0	0	0	0	0	2

In fact a couple balls were hit pretty well in this game, though they were caught. That's what I mean about a no-hitter requiring a lot of luck and also good fielding by the guys behind you.

There wasn't a lot of pressure on me in the game. We got off to a five-run lead in the first inning and the game was never in doubt. We won, 11–0. But I had good stuff, about as good as I've ever had except for maybe two or three other games.

The funny thing is I started thinking no-hitter in the first inning. Why, I'm not sure. It just happened.

Anybody who tells you he wasn't aware he had a no-hitter going is a liar. You always know when you've given up that first hit. As the game went on that day I knew I hadn't been touched for one.

I did walk three men and I think another man got on when I threw a wild pitch for a third strike. But, like I said,

I had good stuff. I struck out 10 men.

There weren't really any tough chances in the field until the seventh inning. Milt May hit a deep fly to left-center, but I didn't think it was hit hard enough. Jose Cruz caught up with it and jumped up to grab the ball.

In the eighth Dave Cash hit a tough hopper toward third base. Joe Torre came in on the run, stabbed the ball and beat Cash to first with his throw.

I figured by the ninth inning that since I had come that far without a hit I really had a chance to make it. I don't remember the first two outs, but I do remember the last one: I threw a fastball past Willie Stargell for strike three and that was the game.

The beautiful thing about the game at that moment was the timing. It came when we needed another win over the Pirates to move up on them in the pennant race.

We didn't win that year, so that part

of it isn't important any longer. What's important now is that it was a no-hitter, something I'd never expected to pitch and could never seriously figure on doing. It's just something that happens, and I'm glad it happened to me.

> . . . YOU NEVER GO OUT THERE AND SAY YOU ARE GOING TO PITCH A NO-HITTER. IT CAN'T BE DONE.

TOMMY JOHN
BACK FROM THE BRINK

OCTOBER 8, 1977

✕

AS TOLD TO AL DOYLE, *BASEBALL DIGEST*, MAY 2004

Its formal term is ulnar collateral ligament reconstruction. But since Dr. Frank Jobe performed the first one on September 25, 1974, it's been known only as "Tommy John surgery," and it has rescued countless pitching careers.

John was in his 12th year when he went under the knife. He'd go on to pitch 14 more, including three 20-win seasons in his first five years after the surgery. When he retired, at 46 years old, he had 288 wins, a 3.34 ERA and 4,710.1 innings pitched, which is 20th all time.

Here, John speaks of that original surgery and how a victory over the Houston Astros in 1976 proved he had successfully returned from radical procedure. But his most memorable game came the following season when he punched the Dodgers' ticket to the 1977 World Series after beating the Philadelphia Phillies in a best-of-five NLCS. It was just his second career postseason start, and he was facing fellow lefty Steve Carlton, who would beat out John for the Cy Young Award that year.

A first-ballot Hall of Famer in 1994 Carlton has the second-most wins by a left-handed pitcher (behind Warren Spahn) on the all-time list. John is ranked seventh.

—SM

DODGERS PITCHER
TOMMY JOHN

Everyone knows about my ligament transplant. I was pitching for the Dodgers in 1974, and I was 13-3 when the ligament was torn.

Dr. Jobe told me what he was going to have to do. No pitcher had ever had that kind of operation before. There was no downside, though, since Dr. Jobe told me, "If you don't have it done, you'll never pitch again."

There was no rehab protocol then like there is now. I was flying by the seat of my pants. I squeezed a ball of Silly Putty constantly and gripped a golf club. The funny thing is that as archaic and primitive as the rehab was, I came back and pitched in the Instructional League a year and a day after the surgery. That's about what they're doing now. The thing I'm proudest of is that I pitched another 14 years and never missed a start because of the elbow.

My first game back with the Dodgers was against the Atlanta Braves on April 16, 1976. It was lackluster and pretty forgettable. I gave up three runs in five innings and lost. Manager Walt Alston called me in the next day and said, "You're going to have one more start and we'll decide what to do with you."

Then I pitched against J.R. Richard and the Astros and shut them out for seven innings. Since J.R. was shutting us out, too, I left with the scored tied, 0–0. But that was the game that showed I could pitch again. I won more games after the surgery than I had before the injury, and I finished the season with 10 wins and a 3.09 ERA.

Exactly three years after the operation — September 25, 1977 — I won 20 games for the first time.

My most memorable game was Game 4 of the 1977 National League playoffs in Philadelphia. We had come back in the third game from being down 5–3, and we were down to our final strike before we rallied. Vic Davalillo was pinch hitting and he dropped a perfect bunt off Gene Garber. Manny Mota came in and had a pinch-hit double off Greg Luzinski's glove. Davalillo scored and Manny went to third. He scored the tying run on an error. The Phillies made another error, and Bill Russell's hit won the game. What a finish!

We were now up two games to one, and I was pitching against Steve Carlton. It rained almost all day and the game started late. We played that fourth game in a virtual rainstorm.

I didn't realize it was raining that hard until I saw a tape of that game. It was pouring in the ninth inning. I struck out Bake McBride to end the game, and we were in the World Series.

Considering the circumstances — a hostile crowd, going against a future Hall of Famer, the rain and wetness and being a sinkerballer on Astroturf — it was probably the best game I ever pitched.

I was fortunate enough to pitch in other playoff and World Series games, but I'll never forget that one.

OCTOBER 8, 1977
BOXSCORE

	1	2	3	4	5	6	7	8	9	R	H	E
LOS ANGELES DODGERS	0	2	0	0	2	0	0	0	0	4	5	0
PHILADELPHIA PHILLIES	0	0	0	1	0	0	0	0	0	1	7	0

GOOSE GOSSAGE

RELAXED AND READY

OCTOBER 2, 1978

AS TOLD TO AL DOYLE, *BASEBALL DIGEST*, MAY 2005

At 6-foot-3, Rich "Goose" Gossage was an intimidating presence on the mound. He had 100 mph heat and never backed down from any batter, so it's interesting to hear in this recollection how he needed to do a little mental gymnastics to complete the save in the "Bucky Dent Game."

Gossage had 26-save seasons with both the Chicago White Sox and Pittsburgh Pirates early in his career. But his most memorable work was in New York and San Diego. Nearly half of his 310 saves came with Yankees, including a career-high 33 in 1980, three years after he joined the team. He had another 83 with the Padres over four seasons after signing as a free agent in 1984.

After he was traded in 1988 Gossage became a journeyman, playing for six teams over his final seven seasons. He retired in 1994 at 43 years old.

Gossage led the American League in saves three times, including the Yankees' incredible comeback year of 1978. He also played on nine All-Star Teams: six in the American League and three in the National. Known as an old-school relief pitcher, Gossage was inducted into the Hall of Fame in 2008.

—SM

What's the biggest game I ever played? That's easy. It was the one-game tiebreaker against Boston at Fenway Park in 1978.

That was my first season with the Yankees, and we never expected to be in that situation. We were 14 games behind the Red Sox in July. Who could have guessed the season would end with a one-game tiebreaker? To play 162 games and have identical records and then go into Fenway with everything riding on one game almost didn't seem fair to the losing team.

Ron Guidry started for us. He had 24 wins and was almost unhittable. Mike Torrez pitched for the Red Sox, and everyone knows the story of that game.

We were losing, 2–0, when Bucky Dent came up for us with two on and two out in the top of the seventh inning. Torrez threw one over the plate, and Bucky hit it just over the Green Monster for a three-run homer. We got another run when Mickey Rivers walked and stole second and Thurman Munson hit a double that scored Rivers.

Guidry gave up a hit in the bottom of the seventh, and Bob Lemon brought me in to finish up. Closers went longer than an inning back then. We were used to pitching in the seventh and eighth. No one had heard of pitch counts. That's garbage.

The night before the game I was already thinking that I might be facing "Yaz" (Carl Yastrzemski) with the game on the line. It's not that Yaz gave me much more trouble than any other hitter. I thought about facing him because he was such a great clutch hitter.

It might have been the biggest game of my life, but it wasn't my best performance. After Reggie Jackson hit a solo homer in the top of the eighth to give us a 5–2 lead, I gave up RBI singles to Yaz and Fred Lynn to make the score 5–4.

I was a bundle of nerves on the mound, and I was having a great conversation with myself. It went like this: This is what you went to bed thinking about last night. Well, here it is.

The Red Sox didn't quit in the ninth. Rick Burleson got a walk, and Jerry Remy hit a soft liner to right. Lou Piniella couldn't see the ball because of the sun, but he still got it on one bounce and kept Burleson at second. Then Rice hit a fly ball that moved Burleson to third.

Yaz stepped to the plate with two out and the game on the line. I started talking to myself: Why are you so nervous? This is supposed to be fun. What's the worst thing that could happen? If you lose you'll be back home in Colorado hunting elk.

After that I felt like the weight of the world was lifted from me, and I was

RICH GOSSAGE

throwing harder than I had all day. On a 1-0 pitch I threw a fastball right down the middle that tailed in hard on Yaz, and he popped out to Graig Nettles at third.

We won the game and the division. We beat the Royals to get to the World Series and then beat the Dodgers in six games to repeat as world champions. But that game in Fenway is the one I'll always remember.

It was total chaos in that tiny Fenway clubhouse. I went into the trainer's room to catch my breath for a minute, and Thurman came in and said, "Where did you get that last pitch? It had another foot on it."

It came because I finally relaxed on the mound.

OCTOBER 2, 1978
BOXSCORE

	1	2	3	4	5	6	7	8	9	R	H	E
NEW YORK YANKEES	0	0	0	0	0	0	4	1	0	5	8	0
BOSTON RED SOX	0	1	0	0	0	1	0	2	0	4	11	0

DAVE STIEB
ALL-STAR EFFORT

JULY 6, 1983

AS TOLD TO GEORGE VASS, *BASEBALL DIGEST*, MARCH 1993

Dave Stieb was the first homegrown star of the Toronto Blue Jays. He was originally drafted as an outfielder in 1978 but was blessed with such a naturally lethal slider that he was converted into a pitcher. He spent nearly his entire career in Toronto, except for a short stint with the Chicago White Sox in 1993. In his 15 years with the Blue Jays he won an impressive 175 games — 140 of them in the 1980s, second only to Jack Morris (162).

When he spoke to George Vass in March 1993, it was five months after Toronto had won the first World Series by a team not based in the United States. Stieb, a fierce competitor who wanted the ball in big games and would not back down from any batter, was injured and didn't get a chance to pitch in the Fall Classic.

Stieb is perhaps best known for his near misses of perfect games and no-hitters, which rendered his 1986 autobiography Tomorrow I'll Be Perfect *a bit ironic until he no-hit the Cleveland Indians in 1990. But it was stopping the American League's All-Star Game misery that he recalls most.*

—SM

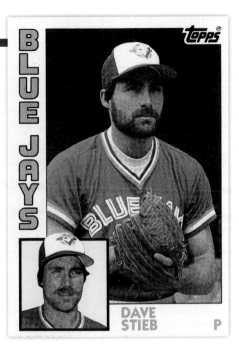

DAVE STIEB
P

hrowing a no-hitter is right up there among the best games of my career. When I eventually got one in 1990 against the Cleveland Indians, I felt like my luck had finally turned.

I can't really say I was nervous going into the ninth inning of the no-hitter. It crossed my mind what had happened the other times. I had five one-hitters in my career — three of them in the 1988 season alone. The last two that year came against Cleveland and Baltimore in my final two starts of the season, and both times I took no-hitters all the way to two outs in the ninth inning. Julio Franco spoiled the first one with a bad-hop single to second. Six days later Jim Traber did the same thing with a bloop single to right. Luck just went against me. The funny thing is that in my no-hitter against the Indians, my stuff wasn't as good as it was in the other games. It was just meant to be, I guess.

If I had to choose my greatest day, though, it would have to be the 1983 All-Star Game. Not that it was all that great a game, being a blowout, but just being part of it — that's what makes it stand out.

I was the starting pitcher for the American League in old Comiskey Park in Chicago, and that meant a lot to me. I went to college in Illinois (Southern Illinois University) and winning an All-Star Game in Comiskey Park, where I'd gotten my first shutout in the majors and where I'd had the most success on the road, all fit together in my mind.

There are a lot of special things about being in the All-Star Game. You get to know the players around the league a little better personally, and then there's the feeling when you take the mound that you've got the best players in the league behind you. You wish that kind of talent were out there every day when you were pitching. Still, you're bound to be a little nervous, and I was.

Comiskey Park was full like I'd never seen it before. The sun was out when the game started and it was shining in the face of the first base-man, Rod Carew. When I picked up a bunt in the first inning and threw it high, it went over his head for an error. Carew never saw it. Another ball hit him right in the glove, but he didn't see it and couldn't hold onto it. The National League ended up scoring a run in the first on no hits and two errors because of the sun.

It was a pretty ugly way to start the game, but things got better. We tied it with a run in our half of the first, scored another in the second and then broke the game wide open in the third with seven runs, four on a grand slam by Fred Lynn.

We won the game, 13–3, and I didn't give up a hit in my three innings as a starter.

Winning an All-Star Game may not be all that meaningful, and I don't think the outcome of the game indicates one league is better than the other. But that game meant a little more than most because the American League had lost 11 straight All-Star Games, so it was a big deal for us to stop that losing streak. And it meant a lot to me personally to be the winning pitcher. It's an honor to be chosen to an All-Star team and you want to live up to the expectations. You want to go home a winner.

JULY 6, 1983

BOXSCORE

	1	2	3	4	5	6	7	8	9	R	H	E
NL ALL-STARS	1	0	0	1	1	0	0	0	0	3	8	3
AL ALL-STARS	1	1	7	0	0	0	2	2	X	13	15	2

ROGER CLEMENS
MOWING THEM DOWN

APRIL 29, 1986

⬠

AS TOLD TO GEORGE VASS, *BASEBALL DIGEST*, JUNE 1990

*Only 13,414 fans were at Fenway Park to witness Roger Clemens'
single-game strikeout record of 20, set in 1986. But the crowd was
boisterous, as he recounts here. His feat has been matched three times
— once by Clemens himself a decade later — but never surpassed.
His 4,672 strikeouts are the third most in history, and he is the only
pitcher to win seven Cy Young Awards.*

*In this 1990 recollection Clemens wonders if he'd ever win a World
Series. His only trip to the Fall Classic had been in that magical '86
season when he went 24-4 with a 2.48 ERA in and won his only AL
MVP. He started five games that postseason, including Game 6 of
the World Series against the New York Mets when the Red Sox came
within one out of their first championship since 1918. Clemens would
eventually win two World Series, though both would come with the
New York Yankees, the archrival of the Red Sox.*

*Although Clemens' game-day paraphernalia from his first 20-strikeout
night is in the Hall of Fame, "The Rocket" is still not enshrined in
Cooperstown for his 24-year career, mainly because of accusations
surrounding the use of performance enhancing drugs.*

—SM

Roger Clemens delivers a pitch during his dominant 1986 season.

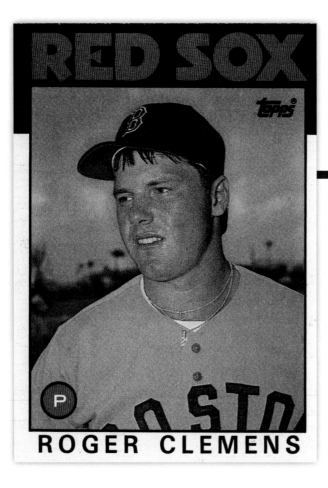

RED SOX

1986 Topps; #661

ROGER CLEMENS

No matter what happens for the rest of my career, I'm in the Hall of Fame. That's something no one can take away from me. But the strange thing about it was that during the game that put me in the hall I really wasn't aware what was happening. I was just concentrating on pitching the best I could in that game.

Hopefully I've got a long career ahead of me and there will be many more high spots, like winning a World Series game and being on a World Series winner. But there have already been a lot of moments to remember, games that I'll probably think about years from now.

They say most players don't really sit back and think about what they've accomplished until they're retired because they're too wrapped up in what's going on while they're playing. But once in a while, mostly when people ask you about it, you do think about what's been happening and what you've accomplished.

Some of the highlights up to now have been being the winning pitcher in an All-Star Game (1986) and pitching in the American League playoffs in 1986 and 1988, and the World Series in '86. I started the seventh game of the ALCS against the California Angels and being the winning pitcher in a game like that is hard to top because of what it means to the team and what it means individually. It's really the culmination of a season of effort, something everybody has been working toward.

There's really nothing in baseball to match getting into the World Series and, for a pitcher, starting a game in the Series. It was disappointing the way things turned out. But I guess it was the Mets' turn and you've got to give them credit — they came back and won it.

Losing that Series was just about the only disappointing thing about '86. It was sort of a miracle year for me, especially because just the year before I'd had surgery to remove a piece of cartilage from my right (throwing) shoulder.

Some people thought I might have trouble coming back from the surgery, but it was never a question in my mind. I knew my shoulder wouldn't be a problem, and I guess '86 proved that.

And I'm sure the game in which I struck out 20 men set any lingering doubts to rest.

APRIL 29, 1986

BOXSCORE

	1	2	3	4	5	6	7	8	9	R	H	E
SEATTLE MARINERS	0	0	0	0	0	0	1	0	0	1	3	1
BOSTON RED SOX	0	0	0	0	0	0	3	0	X	3	8	1

In that big strikeout game against the Seattle Mariners, at first I was just trying to establish my pitches, and in the first inning I ran the count to 3-2 on all three batters before they struck out.

But from the second inning on, things fell into place for me. And I knew I had only fastball and breaking pitches.

I kept getting the strikeouts, and the thing about it was that nobody scored early for either team. When you're in a 0–0 situation like that it makes you sharper. You know you can't afford to make a mistake.

I made one to Gorman Thomas in the seventh inning, and he hit a home run that put them ahead, 1–0. But we came back in the bottom of the inning when Dwight Evans hit a three-run homer.

That gave me a 3–1 lead to work with. It was about that point that I became aware of what was going on. It was a small crowd but a noisy one,

and every time I struck a man out they cheered.

I wasn't sure what they were screaming about until (pitcher) Al Nipper came over to me after the top of the eighth. He said, "Man, Rocket, you've got a chance for an all-time record. Go for it with gusto."

"Nip" had seen the scoreboard flash that I had 18 strikeouts at that point.

I was tired, but the adrenaline was flowing, and I was pitching on that in the ninth. I just threw the ball down the heart of the plate. I struck out the first batter (Spike Owen) to tie the record and then Phil Bradley was called out (on a 2-2 pitch) for number 20 to set the new record.

When Bradley struck out, (third baseman) Wade Boggs came over and shook my hand and I thought, hey, the game is over. It wasn't, but the last batter grounded out and then it was.

Everybody mobbed me on the mound, but it just didn't sink in what it all meant, not right away.

My teammates were all excited, and when I got home I got calls from a lot of my family, most of whom live in Houston. Everybody was crying — my brothers, my mother — and they kept saying, "You're in the Hall of Fame. Nobody's ever struck out 20 in the major leagues before."

They were right. A day or two later the Hall of Fame asked for my glove, spikes and cap, and they wanted the ball I threw past Bradley for the 20th strikeout.

It took a while for it all to sink in. Records are made to be broken, and I broke one. But somebody might come along and strike out 21 batters some day.

But whatever happens I did something no major league pitcher had done before in nine innings, and I'll surely remember it forever.

DENNIS ECKERSLEY

GIANT SLAYER

OCTOBER 28, 1989

✕

AS TOLD TO GEORGE VASS, *BASEBALL DIGEST*, FEBRUARY 1992

Dennis Eckersley was the first pitcher in MLB history to have both a 20-win season and a 50-save season. He won 20 games with the Boston Red Sox in 1978. He was 23 years old at the time and just entering his prime, but it would remain his best year as a starter.

In 1987, after two-plus seasons with the Chicago Cubs, Eckersley was traded to the Oakland A's, where manager Tony LaRussa turned him into a reliever at the age of 32. Eckersley soon became the game's dominant reliever, with 220 saves between 1988 and 1992. He registered a stunning 51 saves in 1992. It was a performance that won him both the American League's MVP and Cy Young awards.

The A's were in the World Series in Eckersley's second season with the club, and that is where he coined the phrase "walk off homer" after giving up the famous Kirk Gibson shot in Game 1 of the Fall Classic. A year later Eckersley finally got his championship ring. It wasn't his best season individually, but closing out Game 4 against the San Francisco Giants remains the high point of his career.

—SM

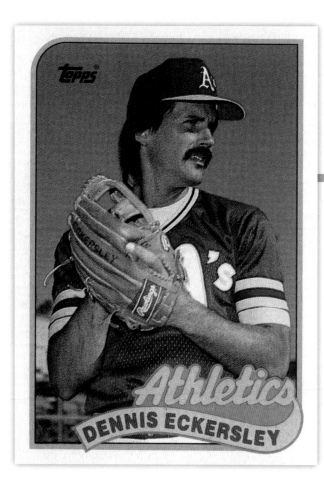

1989 Topps; #370

I've been fortunate to pitch 17 years in the major leagues. Not many pitchers last that long. I've had my ups and downs, but somehow I've always bounced back.

I've got a lot of memories, too, both good and bad. That goes with the job. That and the pressure: one bad pitch and you're in the dumps, one good pitch and you're sitting on top of the world. Anybody who says he doesn't feel the pressure is kidding you. It's always there, whether you're a starter or a reliever. And I've been both. The only difference is that when you start you only face the pressure every fifth day. As a reliever, the pressure comes four or five times a week.

Some managers say, "Go out and play and have some fun." Who are they kidding? Playing baseball is work, it's pressure. I'm not complaining, though. I wouldn't trade being a baseball player for anything.

There's winning and there's losing — to me it makes all the difference in the world. Losing is brutal. It leaves you empty, drained, feeling like you've been stepped on. But you've got to ride it out, remind yourself that it's all part of the game, that things will turn around. All the same, it hurts. I'm not a good loser.

There are a lot of games I'll never forget, some of which I'd just as soon not think about, others that still give me goose bumps.

There's the no-hitter I pitched against the California Angels in 1977

when I was with the Cleveland Indians. I beat Frank Tanana, 1–0. I was a young pitcher and I was thinking no-hitter every time I went out, from the first batter on. After that, I didn't think about it anymore until I got into the sixth inning. It's part of maturing, I guess.

Then there's my first major league start, in 1975. I was just 20, a rookie, and after I'd been in the bullpen a while, Frank Robinson, the Indians manager, gave me a start. I shut out the A's, the world champions, on three hits.

After the '77 season, the Indians traded me to the Boston Red Sox and I won 20 games there in '78. We were in first place most of the year, then lost the tiebreaker to the New York Yankees, the game in which Bucky Dent hit the home run.

That hurt, but I didn't feel it as much at the time as I would have later. When you're young, you think there'll be plenty of opportunities to get to

BOXSCORE

	1	2	3	4	5	6	7	8	9	R	H	E
OAKLAND ATHLETICS	1	3	0	0	3	1	0	1	0	9	12	0
SAN FRANCISCO GIANTS	0	0	0	0	0	2	4	0	0	6	9	0

the World Series. Besides, I'd won 20 games even if we hadn't won a pennant, and at the time I was focused more on individual goals than I was later.

In 1984 I was traded to the Chicago Cubs. We won the division that season, and I lost a playoff game. We didn't get into the World Series, and it was downhill for me there from there on.

In the spring of 1987 I got my act together again, both my arm and my personal life, and I was all geared up for a great season in Chicago. But the Cubs traded me to the A's. I couldn't have asked for a better deal, though. I was going home. I'd been born in Oakland.

When Tony LaRussa told me he was putting me in the bullpen, after all those years as a starter, I accepted it. The way I'd been pitching in the last few years, with my track record, I didn't deserve to start. What I didn't realize was that it was the biggest

break of my career. It was like being born again.

It took a while before I earned the job as the stopper. But I had the pitches and the attitude. I can sink the ball and I've got a good breaking ball to right-handed hitters. But most of all, I'm aggressive. I go after people and I throw strikes.

All that paid off for me. It worked and by '88 I was the stopper. We had a great team, with good starters and a good bullpen — a team that could win, and did.

When it comes to memories, there's one I'd just as soon forget: the home run Kirk Gibson hit off me in the ninth inning to win the first game of the '88 World Series. I had no excuse. I just didn't get the curveball where I wanted and the guy took me deep. It happens. It goes with the territory. That hurt, and so did losing the series.

Winning is a lot better, and the memory I treasure most is winning the World Series in 1989 over the San Francisco Giants.

If there's any game that stands out for me in my career, it's the fourth game of that series when we completed the sweep. That earthquake just before the third game, in San Francisco, was about to start was something so scary, so awful, that it took an edge off the whole thing. It put everything into perspective. But life does go on.

In Game 4 we were leading 9–6 when I came into pitch the ninth. It may seem a lot easier for a relief pitcher to come in with a three-run lead, but still the pressure's there. This is the World Series, remember. I was all pumped up. I wanted to get it over with, to get that World Series ring.

That final out was the sweetest play ever. Brett Butler grounded to Tony Phillips on the right side of the infield and I hustled over to cover first base. When that throw came to me and I stepped on the bag for that final out of the Series, it was a moment I'll always remember. Nothing can top that.

JOHN SMOLTZ
DREAM COME TRUE

OCTOBER 17, 1991

AS TOLD TO BARRY ROZNER, *BASEBALL DIGEST*, OCTOBER 2014

Like most Hall of Famers John Smoltz had many options to choose from when he talked to Baseball Digest. *His Atlanta Braves had won 14 straight division titles, five National League pennants and the 1995 World Series. But Smoltz picked the seventh game of the 1991 NLCS, largely because it's when the run began.*

In 1991 Smoltz was part of Atlanta's "Young Guns" on the mound, with Steve Avery and Tom Glavine. But they were mostly unfulfilled potential, as was much of the team. The Braves were coming off three straight last-place finishes, and that season had started out much the same. Smoltz was only 2-11 by early July, and Atlanta was 8.5 games out of first place in the NL West.

Thereafter, however, he went 12-2 with a 2.63 ERA as part of the Braves' remarkable 54-28 second-half surge. Smoltz' complete game against the Astros on the final Saturday of the season clinched the division title.

Smoltz then won his first career postseason start in Game 3 against the Pirates. But with the Braves down 3-2 in the series by Game 6 he could only watch and hope for a chance to fulfill a childhood fantasy.

—SM

John Smoltz
delivers a pitch
in the 1991 NLCS.

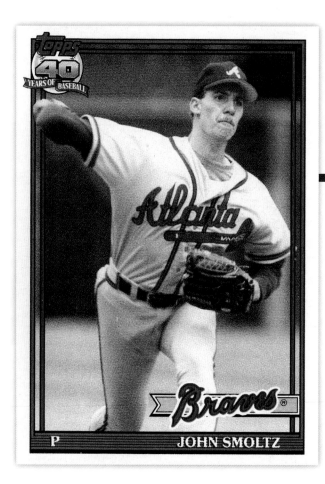

1991 Topps; #157

JOHN SMOLTZ

I felt very responsible for how far back we were in the first half of the 1991 season. We had lost nearly 100 games three years in a row, and all that time I dreamed of winning. I just wanted to know what it felt like to win.

I had a lot to prove personally, and we had a lot to prove as a staff. There was all this stuff about how young and good we were, and there was a lot of criticism from the media about how we would never fulfill our potential.

But we really felt like we had a chance if we caught fire in the second half — and we did. We didn't just come back in the standings. We came back in a lot of games and had a lot of miracle comebacks to win games we seemed to be out of. It was that kind of

team. We never felt like we were out of a game or a series.

The last game against Houston in the regular season was like my first Game 7 because that clinched the division. I went the distance and I'll never forget (catcher) Greg Olson jumping into my arms. Worst to first. Nobody but us believed that was possible at anytime before or during that season. It was a great feeling to be a part of that because I was a big part of why we had such a bad first half.

The 1991 NLCS against Pittsburgh was one of the best series of all time that nobody really talks about. But it was as close as a series can possibly be.

Game 6 was really tough to watch. I had been a nervous wreck ever since I pitched the third game of the series,

and I was just hoping I would get a chance to pitch again. I wanted Game 7 so badly. When we won that sixth game I knew I had the chance to do what I dreamed about since I was a kid — pitch Game 7 to get my team to the World Series.

The day of the game I got in a cab for the short ride to Three Rivers Stadium from the hotel. I was with a couple guys from public relations and I sat in the front seat. Well, the cabbie got in a conversation with the other guys about where we're from and all that. He was very nice, but he proceeded to tell us about how the Pirates were going to get to Smoltz that night and win the pennant. I'll never forget that conversation as long as I live.

We took a 3–0 lead in the top of the first inning and it really took the air out of the place. It was a great start for us on the road, but it gave me a weird

BOXSCORE	1	2	3	4	5	6	7	8	9	R	H	E
ATLANTA BRAVES	3	0	0	0	1	0	0	0	0	4	6	1
PITTSBURGH PIRATES	0	0	0	0	0	0	0	0	0	0	6	0

feeling taking the mound. I was a little out of rhythm right away and I was also a bit nervous because of the lead. Not that a lead is bad, of course, but it just wasn't what I expected.

I started rushing a bit and the Pirates put the first two men on. Then Andy Van Slyke hit a long ball to right field. I thought it was gone. Andy thought it was gone. But David Justice caught it right in front of the wall and I kind of took a deep breath. It was a huge break. I left a fastball up and that could have changed everything, but it stayed in the park. I got lucky on that pitch and another one I threw to Bobby Bonilla, the next batter. After I got Barry Bonds to ground out I felt like we escaped that first inning. I didn't have a lot of experience at that point, and the three-run lead unnerved me. But once I got out of that inning we collectively took a deep breath and the team relaxed.

When I got in the dugout (pitching coach) Leo Mazzone asked me if I was nervous. I said, "Not anymore." And then I told him something like, "Just sit back and enjoy the rest of the game because I have this now." I wasn't trying to be cocky. It was just that I knew. As a pitcher there are just certain things you know. And I knew I was settled from that point on. I was not going to give that ball to anyone. I was finishing that game.

And I did. I was throwing first-pitch strikes and was ahead so often that I was able to use Pittsburgh's aggressiveness against them. Then, with two out in the ninth Jose Lind hit a soft bouncer toward first and I knew it was over. I went to congratulate Olson, who had done such a great job. Then, he kept me alive while the rest of the team mobbed us.

There is no greater feeling. When I was a kid throwing against a brick wall in Michigan I played through Game 7 in my mind so many times, and here it just happened. It was almost too good to be true. It's a moment I'll never forget. I can still feel that feeling today and it's pure joy.

We didn't win the World Series that year, but it doesn't take anything away from what we accomplished, going from last to first. In the World Series we won all three games at home and lost all four games at the Metrodome in Minnesota. We called ourselves the "Outdoor Champs" after that.

People still talk about the magic of that season and what it started in the city of Atlanta. That was the beginning of one of the great runs in baseball history.

I'm just grateful that I got to pitch that Game 7 in Pittsburgh and live out my dream. It really was a dream come true.

JIM ABBOTT
NO-NO PROBLEM

SEPTEMBER 4, 1993

✕

AS TOLD TO AL DOYLE, *BASEBALL DIGEST*, MAY 2007

In the late 1980s the respected weekly Baseball America *chose Jim Abbott as the second-most impactful rookie in the game's history, behind only Jackie Robinson and his 1947 debut season.*

The left-handed Abbott was born without a right hand. He wore a fielding glove on his left hand and during his windup would rest the glove on the end of his right forearm. After delivering the ball toward the plate Abbott would quickly slip his left hand into the glove to field. In his high school and college days, and early in his major league career, batters bunted regularly, suspecting he wouldn't field the ball on time. But that tactic proved fruitless for the most part. He could quickly get his hand back out of the glove to throw out most runners.

Abbott was only the 15th player to make his professional debut (California Angels) in the majors since the draft was instituted in 1965. He overcame incredible odds to make the major leagues, let alone throw a no-hitter. Two years before his no-no for the New York Yankees, he won 18 games for the Angels and was third in American League Cy Young voting.

—SM

1993 Topps; #75T

 y no-hitter against Cleveland at Yankee Stadium is one game I'll never forget.

I had faced the Indians just six days before in old Municipal Stadium, and they hit me hard. I gave up seven earned runs and 10 hits in just three and two-thirds innings. Because of the struggle from the game before I was more focused on throwing high quality pitches.

The Indians had a very tough lineup, with guys like Kenny Lofton, Carlos Baerga, Albert Belle and Manny Ramirez, and I was wild early in the game. The first pitch I threw would have been a wild pitch if someone had been on-base. There may have been some jitters about wanting to do better than I did the game before.

Even though I wasn't striking guys out — I only had three strikeouts in the game — I had a good fastball. Guys were hitting grounders and pop-ups on inside fastballs, and I used a lot of off-speed pitches. My curveball was good that day.

Two double plays helped, and Wade Boggs made a tremendous play going into the hole on Belle. Wade went into a dive, picked it up and threw him out.

Ramirez, who had just been brought up, hit a one-hopper right at Randy Velarde, who made the play and threw him out.

We were still in the race for the division, so I was focused on getting guys out and winning rather than thinking about a no-hitter. The fans really started getting into it in the sixth or seventh inning. Even though it wasn't a huge crowd (27,125), it sounded like the stadium was full.

Those last three innings were really exciting. I knew what was going on, and it wasn't the first time I'd flirted with a no-hitter. There was a game earlier in the year against the Chicago White Sox where Bo Jackson hit a dribbler to center field on a good pitch. You can throw great pitches and not get a break; you don't have much control over the results.

I was focusing on working with Matt Nokes behind the plate, trying to zero in and throw quality pitches. I'll be the first to admit it: my knees were knocking in the ninth inning. I've seen the tape of the game, and I looked a lot calmer than I was.

Baerga came up with two outs in the ninth. I threw a good slider across the outside of the plate, and he hit a grounder to Velarde, who made a nice throw to Don Mattingly.

When the final out was made, it was like time slowed down. It was like someone hit the mute button. Then the sound was turned on loud.

Don came over and gave me the game ball, and everyone congratulated me. Matt was so fired up and encouraging behind the plate that day.

Although it's an individual accomplishment, it takes a team effort to get a no-hitter. Throwing one at the major league level was the furthest thing from my mind.

It's a cherished moment, and one I'll never forget.

SEPTEMBER 4, 1993
BOXSCORE

	1	2	3	4	5	6	7	8	9	R	H	E
CLEVELAND INDIANS	0	0	0	0	0	0	0	0	0	0	0	2
NEW YORK YANKEES	0	0	3	0	1	0	0	0	X	4	8	0

DAVID CONE
A DATE WITH PERFECTION

JULY 18, 1999

AS TOLD TO BARRY ROZNER, *BASEBALL DIGEST*, SEPTEMBER 2016

The New York Yankees won back-to-back World Series in 1998 and 1999 without losing a game in either Fall Classic. Each season was highlighted by a perfect game: David Wells in 1998 and David Cone in 1999. They were the second and third perfect games in Yankees history.

Cone had thrown only 50 pitches against the Montreal Expos when his teammates bowed to superstition and stopped talking to him after the fifth inning. Paul O'Neill had already made a great catch in right field in the first inning, and second baseman Chuck Knoblauch made a tough backhand play on Jose Vidro in the eighth before Cone struck out the last batter of the inning. In the ninth, after an awkward-looking catch from left fielder Ricky Ledee for out number two, Cone got Orlando Cabrera, the Expos' 27th batter, to pop foul to third on his 88th pitch of the game.

The only other perfect game in Yankees history came during the 1956 World Series. The battery for that game was Don Larsen and Yogi Berra. As if Cone's storybook day weren't magical enough, both were on-hand at Yankee Stadium to throw out the ceremonial first pitch prior to the game.

—SM

David Cone winds up to pitch during the 1998 season.

1999 Topps; #101

The funny thing about that game is that I said something to Don Larsen after the opening pitch about him running and jumping into Yogi's arms. And, of course, I got it wrong. It was Yogi who jumped into his arms. How do you mess that up? I felt pretty dumb at that moment. It was embarrassing and he let me know I got it wrong.

It was a really hot, muggy day. It was 90-plus degrees and steamy as can be, so staying loose was not a problem. I threw a bit underneath the stadium just to keep loose, but it wasn't a big deal because it was so hot.

The fifth inning, that's probably the time you start thinking about the possibilities, and then it's mental gymnastics from that point forward.

You have to try to stay out of your own head. You try not to get ahead of yourself, but it's pretty hard not to.

It's a tug-o-war between taking it one pitch at a time, while remembering there's a game to win, and then thinking ahead to what happens in the eighth or ninth inning. You try to stay in the moment, but you're human. You know what's happening. And it's so quiet in the dugout because no one is talking to you. It's the oddest thing in baseball, because dugouts are so loud and there's so much going on with guys talking to each other the whole game, and now no one will speak to you.

I was anxious because I had been close so many times. When I was with the New York Mets we all wanted to

be the first guy to throw a no-hitter for the franchise. But now I was what, 36 years old? You start thinking this might be your last chance at something like this. My stuff was really good that day and I didn't want to blow the chance. Not exactly the thing you should be thinking about between innings, but then you get back on the mound and kind of settle down and go about your business.

It was a tough play that Chuck Knoblauch made in the eighth inning, and he made it look easy. The crowd went crazy for that play and then the strikeout — that kind of carried me off the field for the eighth. I could actually feel my heart pounding as I walked to the dugout.

With one out in the ninth I got strike one on Ryan McGuire and Joe Girardi called for a cutter in on his hands. Joe was calling this great game behind the plate. It was the ninth

BOXSCORE

	1	2	3	4	5	6	7	8	9	R	H	E
MONTREAL EXPOS	0	0	0	0	0	0	0	0	0	0	0	0
NEW YORK YANKEES	0	5	0	0	0	0	0	1	X	6	8	0

inning and I did not shake him off one time all day, but now I shook him off. I wanted to throw the same fastball and I missed outside. What am I thinking, right? Now I'm going to shake my catcher off? I ended up behind 2-1 in the count.

At 2-2 McGuire poked a soft fly to medium left field and Ricky Ledee came in and made the catch. It was a very scary moment because that field during the day can be hard. He must have lost it in the white shirts because he had to adjust at the last second. I shook my head and took a deep breath.

Then there was one out left: Orlando Cabrera. There's no way to really describe what your body feels like at that moment. The crowd is screaming, the whole world is watching and you're trying to execute a pitch when you can hardly feel anything at all. The adrenaline is flowing and you're fighting to maintain your composure.

It's really odd to feel it.

On the third pitch Cabrera popped it just foul on the third base side. When Scott Brosius caught it for the final out I dropped to my knees. Girardi jumped into my arms and pulled me down on top of him. He told me he didn't want me on the bottom of the pile. He was protecting me. To this day I don't really know why I fell to my knees.

What are the odds that it takes place on the same day as Don Larsen throws out the first pitch to Yogi Berra? That's Yankee magic for you. Things happen at that stadium that you just can't believe could happen anywhere else.

Just about every day someone tells me where they were and who they were watching the game with when they saw it. It makes you feel something very special when people tell you they saw you do something they'll never forget the rest of their lives.

> THERE'S NO WAY TO REALLY DESCRIBE WHAT YOUR BODY FEELS LIKE AT THAT MOMENT . . . TRYING TO EXECUTE A PITCH WHEN YOU CAN HARDLY FEEL ANYTHING AT ALL.

HISTORY IN THE MAKING

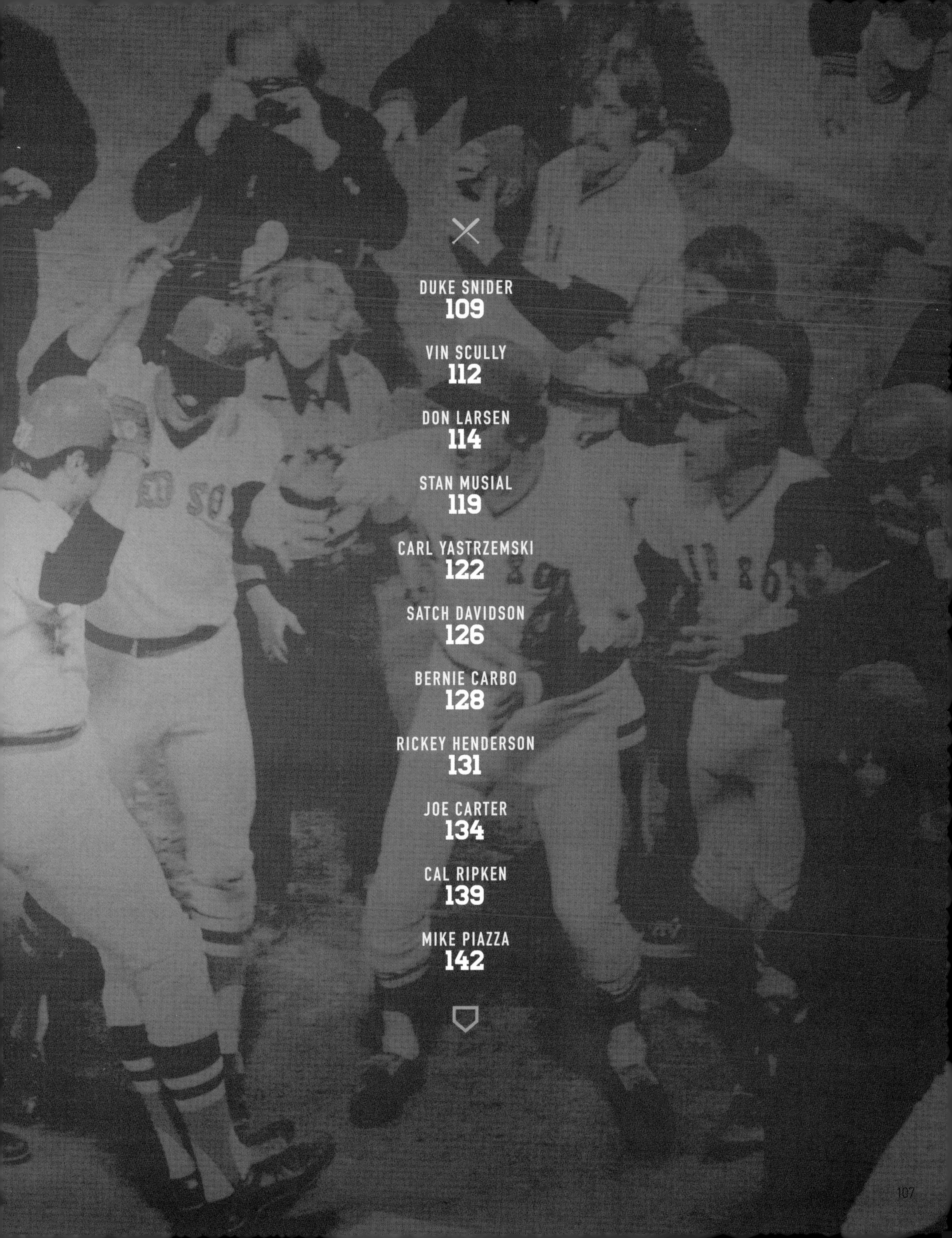

DUKE SNIDER
109

VIN SCULLY
112

DON LARSEN
114

STAN MUSIAL
119

CARL YASTRZEMSKI
122

SATCH DAVIDSON
126

BERNIE CARBO
128

RICKEY HENDERSON
131

JOE CARTER
134

CAL RIPKEN
139

MIKE PIAZZA
142

Duke Snider crosses home plate after smacking his fourth home run of the 1952 World Series.

DUKE SNIDER
CLUTCH PERFORMER

OCTOBER 2, 1955

⬠

AS TOLD TO GEORGE VASS, *BASEBALL DIGEST*, MARCH 1978

In his 1981 hit song Talkin' Baseball, *Terry Cashman's catchy refrain "Willie, Mickey and The Duke" refers to the greatest era (1951–1957) of center fielding ever in one city. New York was home to three teams, all of them with top stars, but Willie Mays of the New York Giants and Duke Snider of the Brooklyn Dodgers vacated the Big Apple when their teams moved west in 1958, leaving the city to Mickey Mantle of the Yankees.*

Snider was five years older than the other two but, like them, was also a five-tool player. He played in six Fall Classics with the Dodgers, winning in Brooklyn in 1955 and then in Los Angeles in 1959. He's the only player to hit at least four home runs in two different World Series ('52 and '55).

The 1955 season, in which Snider was runner-up to teammate Roy Campanella in one of the closest National League MVP votes in history, was immortalized in Roger Kahn's book The Boys of Summer.

Snider, who died in 2011, was the last living Dodger who was on the field when they won Game 7 in 1955.

—SM

1955 Topps; #210

DUKE SNIDER outfield BROOKLYN DODGERS

There are many games that stick out in my mind, but I think the most interesting thing that happened to me was overcoming the insecurity I felt in the early part of my career about ever becoming a real major leaguer.

I had a good season with the Brooklyn Dodgers in 1949, my first year as a regular. I hit more than 20 homers, drove in more than 90 runs and batted .292. On top of that we won the pennant and went to the World Series against the New York Yankees.

But the '49 series was a nightmare for me. I was such a failure. Not only did we lose to the Yankees, I tied Rogers Hornsby's record for striking out (eight times) in a five-game series. I was such a failure that it raised doubts in my mind about whether I'd really be a success as a big leaguer.

It took three years for me to set those doubts to rest. In '51, of course, we lost the playoffs to the New York Giants, when Bobby Thomson hit that home run. Then in '52 we won the pennant again. Even though we lost the World Series to the Yankees, I feel that was the turning point of my career. I hit four homers, which restored my confidence.

Those were the great years in Brooklyn, the early and mid-1950s. I can't think of a better team than the one we had, not with players like Roy Campanella, Pee Wee Reese, Jackie Robinson, Carl Furillo, Carl Erskine and the rest. It was a perfect team for Ebbets Field, which was my favorite park to hit in.

We did well, but there was one hump we could never get over until '55, and that was winning the World Series. Almost every year the Yankees were in our way, and somehow or other they always beat us.

Then came '55, and the game — or games — I'll never forget. I say games because I didn't do all that much in the final one, in which we beat the Yankees to win the World Series for the first time. That meant the most to me, just winning the series. But I've also got to think about the fifth game because I contributed the most to beating the Yankees in that one.

The seventh game is the one in which Johnny Podres pitched the shutout to beat the Yankees, 2–0. I didn't do anything spectacular, but I was involved in a play in the sixth inning that helped produce our second run of the game.

Pee Wee singled off Tommy Byrne, and I laid down a sacrifice bunt to move Pee Wee to second. "Moose" Skowron, the first baseman, fielded the ball, and as I ran down the line

BOXSCORE

	1	2	3	4	5	6	7	8	9	R	H	E
NEW YORK YANKEES	0	0	0	1	0	0	1	1	0	3	6	0
BROOKLYN DODGERS	0	2	1	0	1	0	0	1	X	5	9	2

I brushed the ball out of his glove to reach first safely.

We got a run out of that, because after "Campy" moved the runners along, Furillo walked and Gil Hodges hit a sacrifice fly to score Pee Wee from third.

That was just one of the high spots in that game, the one in which Sandy Amoros in left field made that great catch on Yogi Berra's sinking fly to start a double play and end a Yankee rally. That game brought us our first championship, so in that way it was the greatest I've ever been involved in.

I can't overlook the fifth game, though, because it was one of the greatest days of my career from a personal standpoint. It was certainly a game I'll never forget.

The Series with the Yankees was tied 2-2, and we were playing in Brooklyn. Bob Grim was the Yankee pitcher, and Roger Craig started for us.

We'd lost the first two games of the Series and then won the next two. At that time no team ever had lost the first two games of a Series and come back to win.

I'd hit two homers in the first four games, giving me seven for my career in the World Series. Before I came to the ballpark that day someone told me I had a chance of tying Joe DiMaggio, who had eight home runs in World Series play.

Ever since I was a kid, Joe had always been an inspiration to me, as a center fielder and a hitter. I always considered him to be one of the greatest ballplayers ever to put on a uniform. Even to be mentioned in the same sentence with him was a boost for me.

Strangely that season, until the World Series, I hadn't hit a homer since Labor Day. All I can say is that I wasn't really shooting for homers after we clinched the pennant. But when the World Series came along I realized there was a job to do.

That Yankee pitcher, Grim, had good stuff. In the third inning he threw me as good a curve as I've ever seen.

It came inside and I was lucky to get good wood on it. I hit it over the right field screen to boost our lead to 3–0.

My next time at bat, in the fifth inning, Grim threw me another curve, this one on the outside. I don't think I ever hit a better pitch. This one sailed over the right-field screen, just like the first homer.

I also got a double in that game. I went 3-for-4 with two home runs.

You can get some idea of how I felt when I hit my second homer of the game and passed "DiMag." You bet I knew it, and it went down as one of the greatest thrills of my career. Later (1959), I passed Lou Gehrig, who hit 10 homers in the World Series. I ended my career with 11.

I won't say that was the happiest day of my career, because that didn't come until two days later when we beat the Yankees in the seventh game to win the World Series for Brooklyn for the first time. But it was a game I'll never forget, and I can't think of a greater thrill from an individual standpoint.

VIN SCULLY
ALL CHOKED UP

OCTOBER 4, 1955

AS TOLD TO AL DOYLE, *BASEBALL DIGEST*, AUGUST 1969

It was poetic justice that in the last home game Vin Scully ever called the Los Angeles Dodgers clinched the 2016 NL West division title. And fittingly the final game he ever called in an unparalleled 67-year broadcasting career was between the Dodgers and the Giants. When he retired Scully was the only direct link remaining between the L.A. Dodgers and the Dodgers who had left Brooklyn for the West Coast, along with the New York Giants, in 1958.

Scully is widely regarded as the best broadcaster in baseball history. He was glib, intelligent and had complete economical command of the English language, as he demonstrates in this recollection describing the unbridled joy of Dodger fans after Brooklyn's only championship.

His first year with the Dodgers came in 1950 while the team was still in Brooklyn. That year they lost the National League pennant on the last day of the season. The next year they lost it again after Bobby Thomson's famous home run. The Dodgers eventually reached the World Series in 1952 and again in 1953 but were beaten both times by the Yankees.

Finally their time came in 1955, and Scully was there to describe all the drama.

—SM

The most memorable game I've seen, and the most emotional, was Johnny Podres' 2–0 shutout over the Yankees in 1955 which gave Brooklyn the only world championship it ever had. It was such an emotional experience because it had been so long in coming, and they had come so close before.

As fate would have it I did the play-by-play on the back half of the game after Mel Allen, the Yankee broadcaster, had done the front half. So I did the most dramatic half of a game in which the drama built up constantly.

Here was Podres, a kid out of Witherbee, New York, who had just turned 23 and had only a 9-10 record during the regular season. He had already beaten the Yankees once, in the third game of the Series, after they had taken the first two games.

Now here he was doing this great pitching in the seventh game. Even though we were in Yankee Stadium you could feel the crowd coming around to his side by the seventh inning.

And Gil Hodges, who had had such a bad World Series in 1952 when he went 0-for-21 and had been frustrated again in this Series, finally had a good day. He drove in both runs in this game.

The biggest play of the game was in the sixth inning. The Dodgers were leading 2–0 when Yogi Berra came up with Billy Martin on second and Gil McDougald on first and nobody out. Yogi hit a high fly to the left-field corner, and Sandy Amoros made a one-handed catch near the railing. If he hadn't been a left-hander, with the glove on the right side, Amoros would never have been able to make that play.

He whirled and made a great throw to Pee Wee Reese, who relayed it to Hodges at first to double up McDougald.

For the last out of the game Elston Howard hit a ground ball to Reese. It was the only time in his career that I saw the tension get to Reese. He didn't make his normal throw, but he wanted to make so sure of the out that he took dead aim and threw. The ball started to rise as soon as it left his hand, but Hodges made a great stretch and pulled it in.

The poor Dodgers finally got some winning money out of the Series.

It was incredible. I said, "There's a ground ball to Reese," but I got an apple in my throat and all I could add was, "Ladies and gentlemen, the Dodgers are the world champions."

Down in the clubhouse, the team went crazy, absolutely wild. Podres was actually drunk with emotion.

Vin Scully in the late 1950s.

After the game I drove with one of the members of the Dodgers' board of directors to the victory party in Brooklyn. We drove through the Battery Tunnel into Brooklyn about 5:30 in the evening, and all of a sudden it was like V-J Day (Victory over Japan Day). The contrast was incredible.

The bars were giving away free drinks. Women with babies in their arms were dancing in the streets. When we got out of the car to enter the ballroom where the party was being held, the crowd that was lined up behind the wooden sawhorses even cheered me, the announcer. It was just incredible.

OCTOBER 4, 1955
BOXSCORE

	1	2	3	4	5	6	7	8	9	R	H	E
BROOKLYN DODGERS	0	0	0	1	0	1	0	0	0	2	5	0
NEW YORK YANKEES	0	0	0	0	0	0	0	0	0	0	8	1

DON LARSEN

POSTSEASON PERFECTION

OCTOBER 8, 1956

✕

AS TOLD TO AL DOYLE, *BASEBALL DIGEST*, OCTOBER 2003

Don Larsen's account of his perfect game in the 1956 World Series — the only one in World Series history — is pretty matter-of-fact. It reflects the reality that pitchers know it takes help from teammates, as well as a little luck, to keep runners off base.

Larsen's perfect game also demonstrates how impossible it is to predict when one will happen and, especially, to whom it will happen. Larsen's 11 wins for the New York Yankees in 1956 were the most of his career, and two years earlier he'd gone 3-21 for the Baltimore Orioles. Throughout his career Larsen bounced back and forth between the starting rotation and the bullpen. And in New York manager Casey Stengel often didn't reveal his starter until the day before or even the day of the game. The late call was his way of keeping his pitchers on their toes.

Strangely Larsen knew he had a no-hitter going during Game 5, but didn't know he had thrown a perfect game until he'd left the field. After Larsen's gem the Yankees went on to win the World Series in seven games.

—SM

Yogi Berra jumps into Don Larsen's arms after Larsen's perfect game in the 1956 World Series.

DON LARSEN

pitcher NEW YORK YANKEES

1956 Topps; #332

I actually didn't know I was going to pitch that game until I came to the park.

In those days, I started and relieved. I had 20 starts and 18 relief appearances in 1956. We were always available, even when we were starting. Casey would sometimes use you for an out or two if you were a starter. We all did what Casey wanted us to do.

I'd started Game 2 against Brooklyn, and I was wild. I gave up four runs in one and two-thirds innings to the Dodgers, and Casey didn't like that. We lost the game 13–8.

Many times Casey and pitching coach Jim Turner announced the starting pitcher for the next day's game either the day or night before. If by the night before they hadn't made an announcement, then Frank Crosetti, our third base coach, would perform a Yankee ritual of placing the warmup

ball for that day's game in the starting pitcher's spikes prior to game time.

When I came to the ballpark for Game 5, I entered the clubhouse to find the ball in my spikes.

Everyone asks how I felt before the perfect game. I felt confident as I prepared to face the Dodgers because we were in Yankee Stadium and had won eight of our past nine playoff games there. And you never feel bad when you're in the World Series. You've got all winter to rest.

I threw mostly fastballs, with some sliders and a few curves. I never had such good control in all my life as I had in that game. That was the secret to my success. I'd almost rather give up a home run than a walk.

Four of my seven strikeouts that game were called third strikes. I was throwing the ball right on the black of the plate.

I opened the game by striking out the first two batters, "Junior" Gilliam and Pee Wee Reese, on called third strikes. Then Duke Snider hit a soft fly to right fielder Hank Bauer. Retiring the Dodgers in order helped build my confidence and I was more relaxed on the mound.

Brooklyn had a tough lineup from top to bottom. After Gilliam, Reese and Snider, they had solid hitters in Jackie Robinson, Gil Hodges, Sandy Amoros, Carl Furillo and Roy Campanella. Campanella was batting eighth in the Dodgers lineup, so that gives you an indication of the quality hitters they had.

I retired the first 11 batters before Snider came up for his second at-bat and hit a ball deep to right field. It would've been a home run, but it went foul. I then caught him looking at a slider for my fifth strikeout.

BOXSCORE

	1	2	3	4	5	6	7	8	9	R	H	E
BROOKLYN DODGERS	0	0	0	0	0	0	0	0	0	0	0	0
NEW YORK YANKEES	0	0	0	1	0	1	0	0	X	2	5	0

In the fifth inning Mickey Mantle made a great catch on a ball Hodges hit to the deepest part of left-center field. Mickey also got our first hit — a homer off Sal Maglie in the bottom of the fourth.

It proved to be all the support I would need. But at the time it was just a one-run lead in a tight pitching duel. People forget that Maglie pitched a hell of a ballgame that day, too. He gave up only five hits and two runs, but it was enough for us to win the game.

I knew I was pitching a no-hitter, since every pitcher knows when he's throwing one. But I actually didn't know it was a perfect game until someone told me in the clubhouse after it was over. During the game I tried to engage in conversation with some of our players on the bench, but they all avoided me like the plague. That doesn't happen only in the World Series. It's a baseball superstition for players not to talk to a pitcher working on a no-hitter.

Going into the bottom of the ninth I had just three more outs to go to get

it. More importantly, though, we were three outs away from a three games to two lead in the World Series.

Furillo led off the inning with a fly ball to Bauer in right. One out. Campanella followed with a ground ball to second baseman Billy Martin. Two outs. Then Dale Mitchell entered the game to pinch hit for Maglie. On a 1-2 count I got him on strikes for the final out. Yogi Berra jumped into my arms after the last out.

I had my hat, glove and ball from that game silvered. They were sold in an auction a few years ago, and the money went toward my grandson's college fund.

The Yankees never gave me a penny for that game. I got a few endorsements that winter, but nothing like what would have happened today. Just one of the endorsements was in New York. I went on The Bob Hope Show, but I never appeared on The Ed Sullivan Show.

I was surprised when I got my

contract for 1957. Even though I was coming off an 11-5 season and had thrown the perfect game, George Weiss (Yankees general manager) only offered $13,000, which wasn't much of a raise from $12,000. Arthur Richman (then a New York baseball writer), who has been a good friend for a long time, wrote a letter to Weiss on my behalf. Weiss replied with one that read, "If you forget you wrote this letter, I'll forget I received it." Weiss could be a cold person.

The game has changed a lot since those days. There were only eight clubs in each league, and the winner's share was only $8,700 for the '56 World Series. The people in New York were sort of spoiled because they had three teams (Yankees, Dodgers and New York Giants) and the World Series was played there almost every year.

We ended up winning the 1956 World Series in seven games, but Game 5 is the one I'll never forget.

Stan Musial strokes his 3,000th hit in a matchup against the Chicago Cubs at Wrigley Field.

STAN MUSIAL

THE HUNT FOR 3,000

MAY 13, 1958

AS TOLD TO GEORGE VASS, *BASEBALL DIGEST*, APRIL 1973

Astonishingly Stan Musial, who missed the 1945 season while serving in the navy, hit .310 or higher in his first 17 big league seasons. He won seven National League batting titles, played in 24 All-Star Games and was league MVP three times. He was such a consistent hitter that he had the same number of hits (1,815) on the road as he did at home.

In 1958 Musial was aiming to become only the eighth player to reach 3,000 hits, joining Ty Cobb, Tris Speaker, Honus Wagner, Eddie Collins, Cap Anson, Nap Lajoie and Paul Waner. Musial hoped it would happen in St. Louis, where he spent his entire career, but five hits in a doubleheader left him just two shy of the hallowed mark with a pair of road games coming up against the Chicago Cubs.

Expecting to get the big hit in Chicago, he decided to celebrate early at a restaurant he owned in St. Louis with business partner Julius "Biggie" Garagnani. What Musial wasn't expecting were the impromptu celebrations waiting for him all along the way back to Missouri after yet another clutch hit on the road.

—SM

'58 ALL STAR
Selection

SPORT Magazine

1958 Topps; #476

STAN MUSIAL
FIRST BASE • NATIONAL LEAGUE

I went into the 1958 season only 43 hits short of 3,000, and there was no doubt I would make it without any trouble. The way I had hit in 1957 (.351) it was clear I had two or three more years to go even though I was 37 years old.

But I was in a hurry to get that 3,000th hit. I'd hurt my shoulder in '57 and that had been a warning how suddenly a career could end. The quicker I got the hit behind me the better I would feel about it.

At the time only seven players in major league history had gotten 3,000 or more hits. The last one to do it had been Paul Waner of the Pittsburgh Pirates in 1942; he had been one of my boyhood heroes.

All through spring training in 1958

reporters asked me to set a date when I thought I would get number 3,000. I couldn't do that, of course, but I estimated to myself it would be some time in late May.

Things went even better than I could have hoped for. I got off to a great start, hitting over .500 going into early May. On May 11 we beat the Chicago Cubs twice in St. Louis, coming from behind each time in the ninth inning, and I got five hits.

That gave me 2,998 hits and that night we closed down Stan and Biggies to hold a private party in anticipation of my 3,000th. Our next series was against the Cubs back in Chicago, and with two games there it looked like I might get the hit on the road. That's not quite the way I wanted it. I would

rather have gotten it at home in front of the Cardinal fans in St. Louis.

Just in case I did get number 3,000 in Chicago my wife, Lil, and several friends came along for the Cubs series, which opened Monday, May 12. I got a double in the first game, which left me just one hit away.

After the game I was talking with Terry Moore, one of our coaches, and said, "You know, I hope we win tomorrow, but I'd like to walk four times and save the big one for St. Louis."

Terry must have said something to manager Fred Hutchinson because later "Hutch" called me on the phone in my hotel room. He told me he was going to use me only as a pinch hitter if he needed me. Otherwise he'd try to save the "big one" for St. Louis.

Hutch told reporters, "I'd just hate to see the guy get the big one here when his home fans can have the chance a day later." So I figured that if everything went well the next day I could get number 3,000 in St. Louis.

BOXSCORE

	1	2	3	4	5	6	7	8	9	R	H	E
ST. LOUIS CARDINALS	0	0	1	0	0	4	0	0	0	5	9	0
CHICAGO CUBS	1	0	1	0	1	0	0	0	0	3	7	2

When the second game against the Cubs started on Tuesday, May 13, I was sitting on the bench in the right-field bullpen at Wrigley Field, soaking up the sun.

I stayed there for five innings, but things didn't work out the way I'd hoped. We were behind 3–1 going into the sixth, and we had a runner on second base with a man out when Hutch sent word. He wanted me to pinch hit.

There were only 6,000 people in Wrigley Field that day, but they made a lot of noise when I walked up.

Moe Drabowsky was pitching for the Cubs, and he had been going pretty good until Gene Green got to second base for us with one out in the sixth. The next hitter was our pitcher, so Hutch sent me up to hit for him.

Drabowsky's first pitch was wide. I got a piece of the next two pitches and fouled them off. Then he threw another wide pitch. It was 2-2 and I fouled off the fifth pitch.

His next one was a breaking ball outside. I got good wood on it and the ball went down the left-field line. I saw right away that "Moose" Moryn, the Cubs left fielder, didn't have a chance on it. I never broke stride before I pulled up at second with a double. That was hit number 3,000.

Umpire Frank Dascoli retrieved the ball and gave it to me. Then Hutch came over from the dugout to stick out his hand and offer me his congratulations. He took me out for a pinch runner. I left the field and stopped only to kiss my wife, who was sitting behind the Cardinal dugout, before I went into the clubhouse.

The game was still going on out on the field, but all the press and photographers were mobbing me in the clubhouse. The radio was on, so we could keep track of the score. Finally we won 5–3 and it made the day perfect, especially since it was our sixth-straight win.

Hutch came into the clubhouse and apologized for having used me as a pinch hitter. Can you imagine? "I'm sorry," he said, "I know you wanted to get it in St. Louis, but I needed you."

I wasn't sorry. It was a hit that counted for something, helping to win a game, whether it was number 3,000 or not.

I'll never forget the train trip back to St. Louis on the Illinois Central Railroad after the game. There were crowds of fans at several stops along the way. At Clinton, Illinois, they were chanting, "We want Stan! We want Stan!" when we pulled in. There was another crowd waiting at Springfield. And when we finally got to St. Louis around midnight, there were more than 1,000 people there, too. I had to make a little speech.

That game in Chicago was one I'll never forget, and even if I'd rather had the hit in St. Louis, just getting it anywhere was a tremendous moment in my life.

CARL YASTRZEMSKI
CHASING HISTORY

OCTOBER 1, 1967

AS TOLD TO GEORGE VASS, *BASEBALL DIGEST*, JULY 1974

This memoir is really a confrontation with rarities.

Prior to Carl Yastrzemski clinching both the American League pennant and the Triple Crown on the final day of the 1967 season, only 15 players in league history had led in batting average, RBIs and home runs in a single season. Frank Robinson of the Baltimore Orioles had accomplished the trifecta the year before, but it would be another 45 years before someone else (Miguel Cabrera of the 2012 Detroit Tigers) did it after Yastrzemski.

The Boston Red Sox winning the American League pennant (divisional play was still two years away) was equally as sporadic. The Red Sox hadn't topped the American League since 1946, and Yastrzemski would play in only two World Series (1967 and 1975) in his 23-year career, which is tied with Brooks Robinson for the longest tenure with one franchise. The year before, the Bosox had finished ninth, and in Yastrzemski's first six years, starting in 1961, they had never been higher than sixth. He had also never seen the team draw a million fans, until 1.6 million showed up for the 1967 run, nearly twice as many as there year before.

On the "Impossible Dream" record album of 1967 there was a tribute to "Yaz" that contained the line, "Although Yastrzemski is a lengthy name; it fits quietly nicely in our hall of fame."

—SM

Carl Yastrzemski, left, and Harmon Killebrew show off their bats. Each slugger had 43 homers heading into the final series of the 1967 season.

he game that I'll never forget was played on the last day of the 1967 season, the one in which we won the pennant to bring to life what they later called the "Impossible Dream." It has to be that game, that day, not only because we won the pennant, but also because it capped my finest year with the Boston Red Sox.

Everything seemed to fall into place for me that season, and finishing on top made it perfect. The only disappointment we had was not winning the World Series against the St. Louis Cardinals.

Nobody really figured us to win the American League that year. It was still a 10-team league in 1967, and until July it looked like Chicago, Detroit and Minnesota would fight it out for the pennant to the end.

We started coming on in July, though, and people began taking us seriously after we went into Chicago for five-game series in late August and won three from the White Sox. We were in the middle of things.

We stayed right there through September as each of the four clubs gunning for the pennant put on a surge only to fade back. For a while it looked like the White Sox would win

CARL YASTRZEMSKI • OF

1967 Topps; #355

RED SOX

it, but then the last week of the season the last-place Kansas City A's took two from them in one day.

That put Detroit in good position. The Tigers went into the final weekend with four games at home against the California Angels. If they won all four, they'd have the pennant.

But it rained the first two days in Detroit and the Tigers were forced to play doubleheaders on both Saturday and Sunday, the last two days of the season, which figured to put a strain on their pitching.

Our last two games were against the Twins: Saturday, September 30, and Sunday, October 1, at Fenway Park in Boston. The Twins were in first place with a 91-69 record. The Tigers were a game back with an

89-69 record and we were 90-70, also a game out.

To win the pennant we had to beat the Twins twice and the Angels had to beat the Tigers in at least two of the four games they had left. We won the game from the Twins, 6–4, on Saturday to pull into a first-place tie with them, while the Tigers were splitting with the Angels at Detroit.

There was something else at stake, too, in that Saturday game. Both Harmon Killebrew of the Twins and I went into the game with 43 home runs. I badly wanted to beat him out because I was leading the league in batting and in runs batted in, and if I won the home run title, too, I'd get the Triple Crown. I had three hits, and drove in four runs, three with my 44th

home run. But Killebrew hit a home run as well, so that added even more excitement and pressure, if possible, to the final day of the season.

Everything was on the line for us on Sunday. If we beat the Twins and the Angels could beat the Tigers in one of their two games, then the pennant was ours. Even if the Tigers won both their games, we could force them into a tiebreaker by winning.

The home run title was on the line, too, and the Triple Crown with it. If Killebrew hit his 45th and I didn't, I'd lose the Triple Crown, something few men ever have won.

I didn't get much sleep Saturday night, thinking about what was at stake and worrying about whether I'd be able to hit Dean Chance, a real good right-hander who was pitching for the Twins on Sunday. He'd already won 20 games. Our manager Dick Williams had saved Jim Lonborg, our top pitcher, who had won 21 games, to throw against the Twins.

The Twins got in front 1–0 in the

BOXSCORE

	1	2	3	4	5	6	7	8	9	R	H	E
MINNESOTA TWINS	1	0	1	0	0	0	0	1	0	3	7	1
BOSTON RED SOX	0	0	0	0	0	5	0	0	X	5	12	2

first inning, which was something to worry about with a guy like Chance pitching. They got another run in the third when, with Cesar Tovar on first, I played a single by Killebrew into an error, permitting Tovar to score. You can imagine how that made me feel.

I'd gotten a single off Chance my first time up, but I felt a little better when I got another in the third inning. We didn't score, though, and we were still behind 2–0 when our turn came in the sixth.

Lonborg beat out a bunt to start the inning, Jerry Adair singled and then Dalton Jones got another single to load the bases. I was up thinking we had Chance on the spot. We couldn't afford to let him off the hook.

I waited for my pitch. I figured Chance would come in with a sinker low and away sooner or later. I let the first pitch, a fastball inside, go by for ball one. Now I was ready for the sinker. All I had to do was to meet the ball, not try to kill it.

I guessed right. He threw the sinker, low and outside. I got the bat on it and

lined the ball over the second baseman's head to drive in Lonborg and Adair with the tying runs.

Before the inning was over we got three more runs and had a 5–2 lead. We had all the runs we needed. "Lonnie" gave up another run in the eighth but hung on.

I'd gone 4-for-4 in the last game and Lonnie had kept Killebrew from hitting another home run, so we shared that title with 44. I'd won the Triple Crown with a batting average of .326 and 121 ribbies to go with my 44 homers.

The moment the game was over I sprinted for the dugout. The fans were pouring onto the field, and if they caught me they'd have torn my uniform into shreds for souvenirs. As it was I got pawed all over and felt lucky to escape alive.

But when the game was over we still hadn't won the pennant. The Tigers beat the Angels in the first game and the second was still being played. If they won that, too, they'd tie us with a 92-70 record. We didn't want to have

to play a tiebreaker. You could never tell what might happen.

We all gathered around the radio near my locker listening to the game. The Tigers led early, but the Angels took a 4–3 lead in the third inning. That brought a big cheer from all the guys.

But we didn't feel too confident. That's a small ballpark in Detroit, and it didn't take much to score a lot of runs. The Tigers could do it. We'd had it happen to us there.

The Angels added to their lead and soon they were ahead 7–3. But the Tigers kept hacking away, and it was 8–5 when they came up for their last turn in the ninth.

It was deathly quiet in our locker room when they got two men on with nobody out. The beer and sandwiches were untouched. But the third batter got out, and when Dick McAuliffe hit into a double play to end the game we went wild.

We tore the place apart and it was champagne instead of beer. We'd won the pennant.

SATCH DAVIDSON
WITNESSING HISTORY

APRIL 8, 1974 & OCTOBER 21, 1975

AS TOLD TO AL DOYLE, *BASEBALL DIGEST*, OCTOBER 2005

A bad back forced veteran umpire David "Satch" Davidson to retire in 1984, which, he later told Baseball Digest, *was his one real regret in baseball. But Davidson (his nickname was after a character from the Bowery Boys movies) crammed a lot into his career.*

In his first month in the major leagues he umpired back-to-back no-hitters thrown by Jim Maloney and Don Wilson at old Crosley Field in Cincinnati and was on the field for three more no-hitters in his career. He was also, as he recalls here, the home plate umpire for two of the most famous home runs in baseball history.

The first was when Hank Aaron broke Babe Ruth's home run record in Atlanta. Pictures and films of the mob scene at home plate show Davidson properly positioned a few feet from home plate...making sure Aaron touches it.

In the second Davidson recalls, in detail, watching the seesaw battle between the Reds and Red Sox in Game 6 of the 1975 World Series. And in the bottom of the 12th inning he had a perfect view down the left-field line as he watched Carlton Fisk's legendary home run hit the foul pole in Fenway Park.

—SM

eing a National League umpire for 16 years was a great experience, and I was behind the plate for two of the biggest games in baseball history.

The first big game was when Hank Aaron hit his 715th home run in Atlanta.

It was a bother having to change balls every time Hank came to bat. The stadium was packed before Hank hit the homer. After he broke the record the crowd started leaving. The stands were more than half empty by the seventh inning.

The pitch that Aaron hit wasn't a very good one to pull, but with his strong wrists he put it over the fence. When Hank hit that homer Joe Ferguson (Dodgers catcher) said, "We just saw history."

It couldn't have happened to a nicer guy. I respected Hank because of the way he played and conducted himself. I'd heard about the threats against him, but it's not something you think about when you have to concentrate on the game.

The score? That's not something most people remember: the Braves won 7–4 thanks to the Dodgers making a bunch of errors. No matter what the score was, it will always be the game where Aaron broke Babe Ruth's record.

When it comes to the other game I'll never forget, the score was something that a lot of people have remembered for the past 30 years. I'm talking about Game 6 of the 1975 World Series between the Red Sox and the Reds.

The Red Sox got three runs on a homer by Fred Lynn in the first inning, but the Reds were ahead 6–3 by the eighth inning.

Things looked pretty grim for the Red Sox since they were down 3-2 in the series. Bernie Carbo came up for Boston as a pinch hitter with two on and two out against Rawly Eastwick. Carbo hit his second pinch-hit homer of the series and the game was tied, 6–6.

The Red Sox loaded the bases in the ninth inning with nobody out, but they didn't score. Will McEnaney was pitching for Cincinnati, and with runners on first and third he intentionally walked Carlton Fisk to load the bases.

Fred Lynn came up and hit a shallow fly ball toward the left-field foul line where George Foster came in to catch the ball and threw out Denny Doyle at the plate after he tagged up from third. Rico Petrocelli ended the inning by grounding out to third.

The Reds almost went ahead in their half of the 11th. Joe Morgan drove one over the right-field fence, but Dwight Evans leaped, caught the ball and fired it in to double Ken Griffey off the bases.

Rick Wise came in for the Red Sox

Satch Davidson in 1982.

in the 12th and held the Reds scoreless. Fisk then came up to hit against Pat Darcy, and he hit the famous home run that won the game. When Fisk hit the ball I had a better view of it than the third base and left-field umpires. The ball hit the foul pole and I signaled it was fair.

Pete Rose always liked to talk, and when he came to the plate late in the game he made a remark to Fisk. He said, "I don't know about you, but this is the greatest game I've ever played in."

Even though it was the World Series, you didn't treat it as a special game. You work and prepare the same way every game. Managers and players want to see you hustle, be in the right place, and be consistent. Things go very smoothly if you do that as an umpire.

BERNIE CARBO
FENWAY MAGIC

OCTOBER 21, 1975

✕

AS TOLD TO AL DOYLE, *BASEBALL DIGEST*, NOVEMBER 2005

So much happened in the sixth game of the 1975 World Series between Cincinnati and Boston that, outside of New England, it is easy to forget that without Bernie Carbo's pinch-hit homer there could have been no Carlton Fisk walk off home run.

Carbo had been the Cincinnati Red's first-round selection when the major league draft was instituted in 1965. In 1970, while with the Reds, Carbo was second in voting for the National League Rookie of the Year, hitting .310, with 21 homers, 63 RBIs and 10 stolen bases.

However, it wasn't until he faced his old team in the 1975 Fall Classic that he collected his first post season hits. He knew many of the Reds on the roster in that Series, as indicated in his retelling of his famous pinch hit.

Carbo also had a pinch-hit homer in Game 3, and when he got his first start of the Series in Game 7, he doubled to lead off the first inning, though the Boston Red Sox would go on to lose the game, and the series, 4–3.

—SM

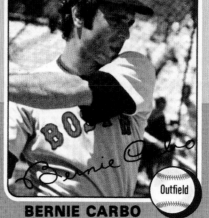

BERNIE CARBO

Outfield

ame 6 of the 1975 World Series — they still remember that in New England today.

We were facing my former team the Reds at Fenway Park, and we were down 6–3 in the bottom of the eighth inning when I pinch-hit for Roger Moret. There were two outs, and Fred Lynn and Rico Petrocelli were on-base.

Even though I was sent up, I wasn't expecting to get a chance to hit. I was a left-handed hitter, and Cincinnati had Rawly Eastwick on the mound, a righty. Reds manager Sparky Anderson pretty much always played things by the book, so I expected him to bring in Will McEnaney, a lefty.

Before I went to the plate, I went over to Juan Beniquez and said, "Get ready to hit," since he was a right-handed hitter. As I went out to the plate I kept looking over at Sparky, watching and waiting for him to bring in McEnaney. When I got into the batter's box, I was still looking at Sparky.

Then I turned to Reds catcher Johnny Bench and said, "Sparky's going to let me hit?"

Before Game 6 we had three days of rainouts. There had been no formal practices or hitting, just some light workouts at Tufts University that I didn't attend. It was the first time I had picked up a bat seriously in all that time.

Eastwick blew the first pitch right by me. I was overmatched, but I worked the count to 2-2 before he threw a slider.

I made one of the worst swings ever. I picked the ball out of Bench's glove and hit a little foul dribbler. Bench said it was worse than a Little Leaguer's swing. Rico said I swung like a pitcher. I was thinking to myself, I almost struck out. My next thought was that Eastwick wouldn't throw another slider.

And he didn't. Instead he threw a fastball on the outside part of the plate. I hit it toward center field, which is pretty deep at Fenway, and started running. I didn't know it was a homer until the center fielder, Cesar Geronimo, turned his back.

Since I was signed out of high school and came up to the majors with the Reds, I knew a lot of guys on the team. When I got to third, I shouted at Pete Rose, "Don't you wish you were as strong as me?" And Pete shouted back, "Isn't this fun? Isn't this the greatest game?" When I touched home plate, I realized the game was tied 6–6.

I went to left field in the ninth. At Fenway, the wind blows foul balls back toward the field, and I almost missed a fly ball that George Foster hit. Dwight Evans made that great catch in the 11th and doubled Ken Griffey off first base, which kept things alive for Carlton Fisk to hit his game-winning home run in the 12th inning.

Even though Don Gullett, a lefty, was pitching for the Reds in Game 7, I started in left field and batted lead-off. I hit a double and scored, and we were ahead 3–0 in the third inning. We thought we were going to win the Series, but the Reds came back to win 4–3.

Some people think Game 6 was the most exciting game in baseball history. How could I ever forget it?

OCTOBER 21, 1975
BOXSCORE

	1	2	3	4	5	6	7	8	9	10	11	12	R	H	E
CINCINNATI REDS	0	0	0	0	3	0	2	1	0	0	0	0	6	14	0
BOSTON RED SOX	3	0	0	0	0	0	0	3	0	0	0	1	7	10	1

Rickey Henderson holds third base high after eclipsing the all-time stolen base record.

RICKEY HENDERSON
MAN OF STEAL

MAY 1, 1991

AS TOLD TO GEORGE VASS, *BASEBALL DIGEST*, OCTOBER 1992

Rickey Henderson — whose uniform was almost always dirty from sliding — recorded a phenomenal 100 steals in just his second year, which was four more than Ty Cobb's 65-year-old American League single-season record for base thefts. Two years later he stole 130, breaking Lou Brock's MLB mark of 118.

Less than a decade later, during his second stint with the Oakland A's, Henderson was chasing all-time records. In 1990 he broke Cobb's 62-year-old American League career mark of 892, and the following year he passed Brock on the all-time MLB list. He would go on to amass a mindboggling 1,406 stolen bases in his 25-year career, nearly 500 more than Brock, who remains second on the list. Henderson is also number one all time in runs scored with 2,295.

If he wasn't getting himself on-base, pitchers were usually doing it for him. Henderson collected 2,190 walks to go with his 3,055 hits. With speed and power — he also had 297 home runs and 1,115 RBIs — Henderson is often described as the best leadoff hitter of all time.

—SM

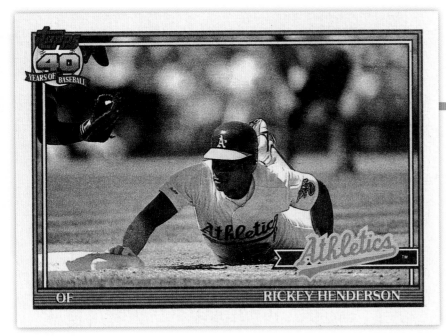

1991 Topps; #670

Nobody likes losing. It hurts every time. To be a good baseball player you have to be competitive, and if you're a competitor you want to win every time you go out on the field. If you don't you're going to be mighty unhappy.

Losing has its advantages, though. Not that you want to get the opportunity to cash in on them too often, but losing can teach you how to win. It can make you hungry enough to push you to the limit so you can win.

I'll never forget the third game of the American League playoff series between the A's and Yankees in 1981, the first time I was with Oakland.

We had chances to win every game if we could have gotten some timely hits. But the Yankees won the first two and we needed to win that third game to stay alive and have a chance to get into the World Series.

In the sixth inning, Willie Randolph hit a home run to give the Yankees a 1–0 lead. That wasn't much, but then things began to go wrong. Our center fielder, Dwayne Murphy, blew out his rib cage swinging at a pitch and, believe it or not, I hurt a ligament in my left wrist doing the same thing.

We were both out of the game and the Yankees scored three more runs to put it away, winning 4–0 and sweeping the series (the ALCS was a best-of-five then). At the time I was 22 and it was a tremendous disappointment coming so close to getting into the World Series.

The other thing about '81 was that after the season I met with Lou Brock and we talked about stealing bases. He taught me so much that his help was one reason I was able to break his record.

I remember meeting with him one day and he told me, "You're going to be the one that breaks my record," which I thought was quite a compliment to give a 22-year-old kid. It set a goal for me, and he made me realize it was possible.

There was a lot of work to be done to improve my base-stealing skills, and I did it all in the years following, with the A's, then for a while with the Yankees, then with the A's again when I was traded back during the '89 season.

There were a lot of big moments along the way, some of which I'll never forget, like winning the AL MVP in 1990, playing on two pennant winners for the A's (1989, 1990) and being on a World Series winner in 1989.

One moment that really stands out was scoring all the way from second on a routine grounder to the shortstop against the Yankees in 1990. We were down 1–0 when I doubled in the eighth inning. I got a great jump off

MAY 1, 1991

BOXSCORE

	1	2	3	4	5	6	7	8	9	R	H	E
NEW YORK YANKEES	1	0	0	1	1	1	0	0	0	4	7	2
OAKLAND ATHLETICS	0	0	3	2	0	1	0	1	X	7	10	0

second when Carney Lansford hit a grounder, and when the shortstop (Alvaro Espinoza) double-pumped on the throw to first, I decided to go for home.

First baseman Don Mattingly could see I was going, but he had to wait for Espinoza's throw and then throw to the plate. His throw home was right on, but I slid in head-first and got my hand on the plate. Something like that you never forget.

It's the same thing about sweeping the World Series over the Giants in 1989, especially with that earthquake in San Francisco. The earthquake was a terrible tragedy, but I think it made the World Series all the more important because it made it more meaningful, taking people's minds off the disaster and showing how life goes on.

Of all that has been memorable for me in my career, though, the most important moment so far has been the game in which I broke Brock's record of career stolen bases by stealing number 939.

A lot has been made of it and a lot of people, especially in the media — which is always looking for controversy — have jumped all over me for a statement I made after I stole that base. They said it was arrogant and out of place. They said I showed disrespect for Brock.

I stole that base May 1, 1991 against the Yankees in Oakland. I reached base in the fourth inning when Espinoza had trouble with my grounder, and I took second on a single by Dave Henderson. After Jose Canseco flied out, Harold Baines came up.

On the second pitch I headed for third and made it. I was so pumped up I tore the bag from its base and showed it to the crowd. Brock, who'd been with us waiting for that steal, came running out on the field and I hugged him then hugged my momma, who also came out there.

They held a ceremony right on the spot and somebody pushed a microphone in my face. I said a lot of things,

among them that "Lou Brock was the symbol of great base-stealing, but today I'm the greatest of all time."

A lot of people resented that. They just ignored what else I said, thanking all the people, including Brock, who'd helped me along the way. They just took that and made it seem I was Mr. Ego, that all I thought of was myself.

It wasn't fair, but it doesn't change anything. It was a great moment for me, one I'll never forget.

LOU BROCK . . . TAUGHT ME SO MUCH THAT HIS HELP WAS ONE REASON I WAS ABLE TO BREAK HIS RECORD.

JOE CARTER
TOUCHING THEM ALL

OCTOBER 23, 1993

AS TOLD TO AL DOYLE, *BASEBALL DIGEST*, MARCH 2014

Joe Carter's 1993 World Series walk off winner is certainly one of the most significant home runs in MLB history, yet it is often overlooked when the best plays in history are recounted.

Only two Fall Classics have been decided by a walk off homer. Bill Mazeroski's solo blast off Ralph Terry in 1960 broke a tie and gave the Pittsburgh Pirates the World Series in seven games, while Carter's three-run blast off Philadelphia's Mitch Williams overcame a one-run deficit to give the Blue Jays the title in six games. When Mazeroski blasted his winning shot, Pirates teammate Dick Schofield was waiting to congratulate him at home plate; incredibly, waiting for Carter after his homer was Schofield's son Dick Jr., Carter's injured Blue Jays teammate.

Out of respect for the way Williams handled the devastation, Carter never went on talk shows to discuss the famous walk off, partly explaining why it doesn't hold a higher spot on most arbitrary "best of" lists.

Toronto was up 3-2 in the series but down 6–5 in Game 6 heading into the bottom of the ninth inning when Carter came to the plate against Williams with two on and one out.

—SM

Joe Carter is hoisted high by teammates after hitting his World Series-winning homer in 1993.

1993 Topps; #350

JOE CARTER
BLUE JAYS

The 1993 World Series was full of the kind of games where you could never relax, even if you had a huge lead. You talk about "no lead is safe." Well, no lead was safe in that Series.

With the Phillies up by a run heading into the bottom of the ninth in Game 6 Rickey Henderson was walking up and down the dugout, telling everyone that he was going to walk on four pitches. That was so Rickey to say that. And then he did it. After that, it felt like a lock that we would score and tie it because Rickey would probably steal second and third. That was a big advantage for us because Mitch Williams had to worry about Rickey running and couldn't focus only on the hitter.

I was trying not to think about how you dream about this when you're a kid — but you dream about this when you're a kid. You're at home plate with a chance to win the World Series. But I hadn't faced Mitch in several years, and my idea was to take pitches until I got a strike. It never bothered me to hit deep in the count, so I was relaxed.

First pitch, fastball up and away. Ball one. Next pitch, fastball up and away. Ball two. He has to throw me a fastball down the middle here, right? He needs a strike. Fastball down the middle for strike one. I'm thinking a base hit scores Rickey and gets Paul Molitor into scoring position, maybe even third base because he's got a great lead off of first. Next pitch is a slider down and in, and I had a terrible swing.

Second baseman Mickey Morandini moved toward the bag and I completely lost the ball in his jersey. I thought it was a fastball down the middle and I just lost sight of it. So now it's 2-2 instead of 3-1, and I had to change my thinking a bit.

Mitch made me look so bad on the slider that I decided he's got to come back with it. I was always a pretty good guess hitter and I figured slider. But then Mitch shakes off the sign from Darren Daulton. I decide in my mind that they're just trying to trick me — that he's still going to throw the slider. I saw Morandini shift back to his left away from the bag. Does that mean fastball? All the rules say you have to look fastball in that situation, I'm still thinking slider and I'm just glad Morandini is not in my line of sight anymore. I figured they were trying to bait me, so I was going

BOXSCORE

	1	2	3	4	5	6	7	8	9	R	H	E
PHILADELPHIA PHILLIES	0	0	0	1	0	0	5	0	0	6	7	0
TORONTO BLUE JAYS	3	0	0	1	1	0	0	0	3	8	10	2

to stay back and try to hit it up the middle.

Mitch was much smarter pitcher than people gave him credit for. He had this reputation as a wild thrower, which he used to his advantage. Guys didn't want to dig in. But he was a *pitcher*. He knew how to pitch and he completely fooled me. He beat me. Turns out I was so wrong on thinking he was going to throw me a breaking ball. He threw a fastball.

It wasn't a bad pitch, but it cut in a bit. Because I was looking for a breaking pitch, and with the way it broke, I was able to get good wood on it. If I'd been looking fastball it would have been strike three, or maybe I would have fouled it off.

When I hit it I knew I hit it well, but I looked up right away and I couldn't find the ball. I saw the big bank of lights in left field. Was it high enough?

Did I elevate it enough? Was it fair? I was jumping all the way down the line, trying to see it, and maybe I was giving it a little body language.

I have so much respect for Mitch. What he did was impressive. He handled giving up a walk off homer with dignity. (He stayed in the Phillies clubhouse and talked until there wasn't a reporter left.) You know, if I strike out there, no one even remembers that at-bat. He's the pitcher, so everyone remembers. It's completely unfair. That's sports. There has to be a winner and a loser. But the difference between those two teams was nothing; like the difference between that home run and a strikeout.

There isn't a day that goes by that someone doesn't come up to me to talk about it. It's very gratifying that people remember you. People tell me where they were when they saw it,

and most of them say they were at the park. SkyDome held about 52,000. But from what I've heard, there were 500,000 there that night.

That's baseball for you.

> YOU TALK ABOUT "NO LEAD IS SAFE." WELL, NO LEAD WAS SAFE IN THAT SERIES.

THE ☀ SUN

2131

LEGG MASON

Bud

Coca-Cola

HIT IT HERE

Cal Ripken takes a lap of Oriole Park in Baltimore after setting the all-time, consecutive-games played mark.

CAL RIPKEN

THE STREAK

SEPTEMBER 6, 1995

◇

AS TOLD TO BARRY ROZNER, *BASEBALL DIGEST*, MARCH 2016

It remains one of the most emotional scenes baseball has ever seen: a 22-minute standing ovation as Cal Ripken did a slow lap, reluctantly at first, around Oriole Park at Camden Yards. He stopped to celebrate with fans and, movingly, reached his fingers through the screen near home plate to touch his younger brother Billy, a teammate when their father, Cal Sr., managed the Orioles.

Ripken had just played his 2,131st game in a row — one more than the original Iron Man, Lou Gehrig, had played. President Bill Clinton and vice-president Al Gore were in attendance, as was Joe DiMaggio, a teammate of Gehrig's.

Ripken's streak began May 30, 1982, and didn't end until he sat out the final home game of the 1998 season. He not only played every day during that time, he played at a higher level than most players — and at shortstop, the very heartbeat of the game.

The 1994 World Series had been canceled because of the players strike, and most baseball historians feel that the stretch run of Ripken chasing down Gehrig helped bring disenchanted fans back to the game.

—SM

1995 Topps; #588

Cal Ripken
SS — BALTIMORE ORIOLES

I just wanted to be a baseball player. I loved playing the game and wanted to be good at all parts of it. I wanted to play every day because I thought that's what you were supposed to do, not because of the record. I didn't really think about it all those years everyone was talking about it. It certainly didn't start off as something I was going after.

At the beginning, when I came up to the majors, you just went to the park and played. Everyone did. That's what we were taught. That's what my dad taught me. You went to the park and played. You were afraid someone would take your job, so you wanted your name penciled in every day. You wanted to be the guy the manager could write down on that lineup card every day.

Managers have a tough job, making out that lineup every day for six months. They try to find a winning lineup and you want them to think you're a winning player, so it's an honor to see your name on the lineup card. A lot of guys played every day, and a lot of guys played through injuries because they wanted to win games and be a part of it. They felt a responsibility.

That's what I felt — a responsibility to be in the lineup every day and try to help the team win games. The streak just kind of happened. For years I ignored it and just played. It wasn't as a big a deal to me as others made it out to be.

I was criticized quite a bit for it, too, but when it got to be near 2,000 games, suddenly it became a positive thing and it was good for baseball. That's when I started to believe there was some meaning to it. But mostly I just wanted to play.

The mental hurdles of being tired in August and September were more difficult to clear than the physical part of the game. You can train for the physical part, but you have to learn the mental part of it. But once you figure out how to put a bad game behind you and get ready to play the next day, you can play every day. That's what I did.

Sure, there were injuries, but every player plays with something wrong. That's just the way it is. Injuries are something you only have so much control over. You can work hard to make sure you're in great shape so that you can play through injuries and avoid them. But some are out of your control, like slides at second base, getting hit by a pitch or collisions.

I didn't think about the streak a lot. It wasn't until I got about a year away from it that I started to think it was possible. Then, we lost the end of 1994

SEPTEMBER 6, 1995
BOXSCORE

	1	2	3	4	5	6	7	8	9	R	H	E
CALIFORNIA ANGELS	1	0	0	0	0	0	0	1	0	2	6	1
BALTIMORE ORIOLES	1	0	0	2	0	0	1	0	X	4	9	0

and the beginning of 1995 to the work stoppage, and it slowed everything down.

When we finally got to the game against the Angels in early September, I hit a home run in the fourth inning. I wasn't trying to do anything special there. I was just trying to get a good pitch to hit and drive it into the gap. I got all of it and it went out. It was kind of magical because it happened that night.

When Mike Mussina got the last out of the fifth to make the game official and they changed the banner from 2,130 to 2,131, I was relieved and excited, but probably relieved as much as anything that it was over.

It all hit me then and it was emotional. It's ridiculous to think of yourself in the same sentence as Lou Gehrig. That's Lou Gehrig you're talking about. It was a bit overwhelming at that moment.

After I stepped out of the dugout to tip my hat to the crowd, I was taking a deep breath and getting it together when Bobby Bonilla and Rafael Palmeiro said I had to go out and take a lap around the field or the crowd would never stop. That's where that came from. It was their idea.

It became a personal moment that I had with all those people in the park that night. It's funny because I saw people I knew who were there every day, who had been there so many of the days I had been there, and that was really the best part about it. It was no longer just this big event, but lots of little small events and it was really a great part of the night. Having my family there, my dad, it was really emotional.

I don't agree with those who say it saved the game. It was something that was good and something fans could feel happy about, but I think it gets overstated. Still I'm glad if it made people feel good about baseball. That was part of my responsibility, as I saw it. I wanted to help the game any way I could. I wanted people to love the game. So if that was a small part of it, I'm happy about that.

> IT'S RIDICULOUS TO THINK OF YOURSELF IN THE SAME SENTENCE AS LOU GEHRIG. THAT'S LOU GEHRIG YOU'RE TALKING ABOUT.

MIKE PIAZZA

HOME RUN HEALING

SEPTEMBER 21, 2001

AS TOLD TO BARRY ROZNER, *BASEBALL DIGEST*, NOVEMBER 2013

Mike Piazza is the only catcher besides Johnny Bench to hit 40 homers during a season in which he caught 120 games or more. He did it twice, in 1997 and '98, and hit 427 of them over his 16-year career. But one in particular stands out for him.

It was just one home run, but for Piazza it was an important symbol. It came during the first professional sports game played in New York after the terrorist attacks on the World Trade Center 10 days earlier. Only a few days before, Shea Stadium had still been a major staging area for rescue and recovery teams.

Mayor Rudy Giuliani wanted the city to return to normality as quickly as possible, and the Mets-Braves game was to be part of that recovery. A number of dignitaries were present, and players from both teams met on the infield before the game, wearing NYPD and NYFD hats. Bagpipers played Amazing Grace *and, in the seventh inning stretch, Liza Minnelli sang* New York, New York.

An inning later, with the Mets down 2–1, Piazza stepped to the plate with one out and one man on.

—SM

Mike Piazza warms
up prior to the start
of a game in 1999.

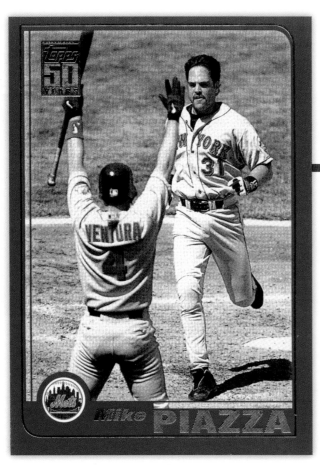

2001 Topps; #706

We had to question whether we should be there to play a game. How could you not, right? It really strikes at your competitiveness. It's tough to really get intense for a game when all this happened around you in the span of a week.

You get frustrated because people refer to us as heroes. Hero is a term thrown around too loosely. I'm not trying to say we don't inspire people, because I was inspired as a kid by my favorite players, but "heroes" means something else to me. We wanted to do our part to help people heal, and the game needed to be played for the good of the city, but we knew it was insignificant in the bigger scheme of things.

I think there are very few times in life when an event happens, good or bad, where you really question your life and it has a deep impact on your soul. For me 9/11 was not only a turning point in my career as far as the game, but also my life. It just caused me to really internalize what life is about, what true love is and how important family and friends are. It shook me to my core.

I was stunned by the magnitude of it. The hardest thing I've ever had to do as an athlete was play that game.

All those emotions we were experiencing through that week came to a head that night. Braves players would come to the plate and we would exchange words or talk a bit, and everyone kind of felt the same way.

It's like we knew we had to do it, but it was hard to get into it. The game is hard enough to play under normal conditions, but under those circumstances it was excruciating.

It was sort of a deep philosophical discussion in your own mind. It made me wonder what life is about and how precious it is and fragile it is, and how there is true evil in the world. I'm a very religious guy and I'm not afraid to say that. When I hear people talk about rationalizing evil it makes no sense to me.

So you hit that spectrum from sadness and fear and despair to anger. It was a very draining range of emotions from start to finish.

We were down 2–1 in the bottom of the eighth when I came to bat with one on against Steve Karsay. It was my fault we were down, because I had made an error on their first run.

That's not how it was supposed to go. We fully expected to win that game. We had to win that game. I knew what the fans wanted, and it

BOXSCORE

	1	2	3	4	5	6	7	8	9	R	H	E
ATLANTA BRAVES	0	0	0	1	0	0	0	1	0	2	9	0
NEW YORK METS	0	0	0	1	0	0	0	2	X	3	8	1

almost felt like a dream to me. It was kind of blurry. I was almost in tears, but I knew I had a job to do and I was torn. I put myself back in the moment and used all of my mental tools to get focused.

Karsay was always very challenging to face, and he always came right after you. I took the first pitch, a fastball, right down the middle and I was very frustrated. I was thinking, that might be the best pitch I get to hit.

I usually take a strike under normal circumstances, but that might have been a pitch I should have been ready for. On the other hand, it was one of those what-ifs. I could have swung and grounded into a double play.

Then he threw the same pitch again, down in the strike zone but across the plate. I was just fortunate that I didn't try to pull the ball. I distinctly remember trying to hit it up the middle, and I'm glad I was able to do what I was trying to do. I usually had decent power to the alleys, so it was something that if I could get the barrel of the bat on the ball, I could drive the ball for extra bases.

I knew I hit it on the screws and that it went out, in left-center, to give us the lead. Other than that I have no recollection of running around the bases. I just remember the surge of emotion. I tried to take it in. My whole demeanor was never one to be reflective in the moment. It's not like I had a mental block. It was just one of those things I can't describe.

I remember holding it together and I remember seeing Robin Ventura at home plate. I got to the dugout and all the guys were on the field waiting. I remember seeing the rush of emotion and seeing all my teammates. I was able to smile and enjoy it a little. My teammates kind of gave me permission to do that.

I remember being in the clubhouse after the game, but I literally went straight home and to bed. I was so exhausted and it was such a draining thing. I was emotionally spent.

To this day I have a hard time looking back and thinking about the game, but the fans have helped me. Every time I'm in New York, regardless of where, people talk to me about that moment and say it may have helped them just a little bit. I'm honored and very flattered. I'm grateful that people put that home run in such high regard. If I were to be remembered for one home run, that to me is the greatest tribute.

You can't rationalize that sort of fear, horror and despair we felt then, but at the end of the day you have to somehow move on. That home run helped me move on. I'll always be grateful to the people of New York for allowing me to do that.

THE HARDEST THING I'VE EVER HAD TO DO AS AN ATHLETE WAS PLAY THAT GAME.

IT'S ALL ABOUT THE TEAM

HANK AARON
148

TOM SEAVER
152

JOHNNY BENCH
156

KEN GRIFFEY
161

ROBIN YOUNT
165

PAUL MOLITOR
168

RICK SUTCLIFFE
172

OZZIE SMITH
176

GARY CARTER
181

JACK MORRIS
184

DAVE WINFIELD
187

HANK AARON
HAMMERIN' IT HOME

SEPTEMBER 23, 1957

AS TOLD TO GEORGE VASS, *BASEBALL DIGEST*, AUGUST 1970

Of course the game "Hammerin' Hank" remembers most involved one of his homers. After all he hit 755 of them in his career and broke Babe Ruth's 45-year-old record of 714 homers on April 8, 1974.

But this memory, recorded four years before Aaron braved serious death threats chasing Ruth's record, speaks to how much the Braves and Milwaukee meant to him. The Braves were still in their final season in Boston when, in June 1952, they signed Aaron away from the Negro American League's Indianapolis Clowns. They offered him $50 more per month than the New York Giants did, or Aaron would have spent his career playing right field beside Willie Mays.

By Opening Day 1954 Aaron was in Milwaukee for the Braves' second year there.

Aaron's Braves, who went to the '57 and '58 World Series, are one of the most underrated teams in baseball history.

Aaron mentions that playing center field for a while affected his hitting. Well that season he hit the most homers (44) of his first eight big-league seasons, had an OPS of .978 and won the only MVP award of his spectacular career.

—SM

Hank Aaron hits a three-run homer in Milwaukee during Game 4 of the 1957 World Series.

1957 Topps; #20

HANK Aaron
MILWAUKEE BRAVES OUTFIELD

That's easy, picking out the game I'll never forget. I can even tell you the date without thinking about it. It was September 23, 1957, the game in which we clinched our first pennant at Milwaukee.

It wasn't just what happened that day that made the game so big in my mind. It was what had happened the year before: we blew the pennant in 1956. We had been thinking about it ever since, and it was making us nervous, a little tight, as the 1957 season got near the end.

There was no two ways about it. We had the '56 pennant in our grasp and then we lost it. We had nobody to blame but ourselves, and we didn't need the fans to remind us of that,

though they weren't hesitant to do so.

We went into the final weekend of the '56 season with a one-game lead over the Brooklyn Dodgers, with each of us having three games left to play. The Dodgers were at home against the Pittsburgh Pirates while we were playing the Cardinals in St. Louis.

The Dodgers got rained out Friday night and we lost to the Cardinals 5–4, so our lead was down to a half game. We still weren't worried. If we won our remaining two games the Dodgers had to win all three (including a doubleheader) to catch us, and we had our best pitchers, Warren Spahn and Lew Burdette, going for us Saturday and Sunday.

It seemed good, but it didn't work out that way. The Dodgers beat the

Pirates twice on Saturday afternoon, and all of a sudden they were a game ahead of us on the win side. We had a night game at St. Louis, so we went into it knowing we had to win.

The Cardinals had a skinny, red-haired pitcher named Herm Wehmeier going for them, and we had Spahn, just about the best pitcher in baseball. When Billy Bruton hit a home run for us in the first inning we began to feel better. But we couldn't seem to do anything with Wehmeier after that, though we got nine hits in the first 11 innings and I had three of them.

Meanwhile, Spahn was pitching a great game, though the Cardinals got a run to tie the game. But they had only three hits going into the bottom of the 12th. That's when Stan Musial doubled and Rip Repulski got another double to drive him in and give the Cards the game, 2–1.

That was it. We beat the Cardinals the next day, but the Dodgers won, too. They had the pennant and we had all winter to think about what

SEPTEMBER 23, 1957

BOXSCORE

	1	2	3	4	5	6	7	8	9	10	11	R	H	E
ST. LOUIS CARDINALS	0	0	0	0	0	2	0	0	0	0	0	2	9	3
MILWAUKEE BRAVES	0	1	0	0	0	0	1	0	0	0	2	4	14	0

had happened. I know I was thinking about it right up to the time we finally did win the pennant in 1957.

I don't know just when we did get into first place to stay that season. It must have been about mid-August, and it wasn't until we had run into some trouble.

Our center fielder, Bruton, got into a collision with our second baseman, Red Schoendienst, around the All-Star Game. Bruton tore ligaments in his right knee and didn't play any more that year. I had to go to play center field, and I'm sure that affected my hitting (that year).

Luckily we brought up a young outfielder named Bob Hazle to take Bruton's place. He and Andy Palko platooned in right field. Hazle had been just a fair hitter in the minors, I guess, but when he came to us he really caught fire. He hit over .400 in something like 40 games and the papers started calling him "Hurricane" Hazle.

We were going good, but right after Labor Day we lost eight of 11 games and the Cardinals started coming at us. Our lead, which had been pretty big, dropped to just two and a half games and we started thinking about 1956.

I know Fred Haney, our manager, was worried because he was pretty down at the mouth. He'd seen teams blow big leads before. But we got turned around and started winning again. We won six in a row and went into that game at home on September 23 against the Cardinals with a chance to wrap it up.

It had been a tough day for me, as my oldest child was sick and my mother had come to help my wife take care of the family. That's one thing I'm glad about — my mother was at the game that day, along with a lot of other people because Milwaukee had been waiting for that day since the Braves moved there in 1953.

Burdette was pitching again and for a while it seemed like it was going to be just like the game the year before. We were tied 2–2 in the 11th inning and Johnny Logan was on-base when I came up to bat. By that time Billy Muffett was pitching in relief for the Cardinals.

I remember looking up at the clock as I stood there waiting for his pitch. It showed 11:34, and that's when I hit the ball over the center-field fence to give us the game, 4–2, and win the pennant.

All the players grabbed me as I came across the plate and carried me off the field. When we got to the locker room Wes Covington (left fielder) was the first one to pour champagne over my head.

My first thought when the ball went over the fence was about Bobby Thomson's home run. That always was my idea of the most important homer. Now I'd hit one myself. I don't get excited too often, but this time I was.

I guess just about everybody in Milwaukee went wild. People were snake-dancing in the streets that night, and the next day I felt like the King of Wisconsin.

TOM SEAVER

ALMOST PERFECT

JULY 9, 1969

AS TOLD TO GEORGE VASS, *BASEBALL DIGEST*, NOVEMBER 1974

Jimmy Qualls played just 43 games for the Chicago Cubs in 1969 and had only 31 hits. His most infamous connection prevented Tom Seaver from a chance at becoming just the 10th pitcher in the history of the majors to throw a perfect game.

In the story Seaver recounts here, the spoiled perfect bid wasn't what mattered. His New York Mets' 4–0 victory was much more important. The Mets were chasing the front-running Cubs, who would spend 155 days in first place until they collapsed late. New York went on to top the NL East, sweep the NLCS and win the World Series. It was the quickest ascension of any expansion team in baseball history.

The 1969 season was considered the 100th anniversary of professional baseball. It was also the first year of divisional play and the first with a 10-inch mound, after decades of pitchers throwing from a 15-inch bump. Seaver finished the season 25-7 with a 2.21 ERA and won his first of three Cy Young Awards. Qualls would play only 20 more games in the majors. Eventually Seaver did get a no-hitter, though it came for the Cincinnati Reds in 1978.

—SM

Tom Seaver winds up for a pitch in the opening inning of Game 1 of the 1969 World Series.

I still get needled about Jimmy Qualls. Even now. "Imagine that, Qualls!" people say. They don't let me forget it. But do I have regrets? Lord, no! When you pitch a one-hit shutout in the middle of a pennant race, that in itself is a very memorable game. No other game sticks out for me quite like that one.

You have to remember the situation in July 1969. The Cubs came into New York on July 8, 1969, 5.5 games in front of us. We were in second place, but the Cubs weren't taking us seriously as contenders. Not too many people were.

Just before the first game of the series Ron Santo, the Cubs third baseman, made a comparison of their lineup with ours, pointing out how in almost every case Chicago had an established star at a position while we had young, relatively little known players.

The Cubs did have a good team — Santo, Ernie Banks, Glenn Beckert, Randy Hundley, Don Kessinger, Billy Williams — and maybe our guys weren't as well known. But Santo totally underrated our ball club. He underrated our defense and he wasn't aware of the kind of pitching we had.

TOM
SEAVER
Pitcher

1969 Topps; #480

METS

We had very strong, very good pitching.

We were young, though, and none of us pitchers— Jerry Koosman, Gary Gentry, Nolan Ryan, Tug McGraw and myself — had been around more than two or three years. So I guess maybe there was room for speculation.

Players will frequently do what Santo did — compare lineups and overlook the importance of pitching. If they do that they're going to be wide open to make a mistake. Pitching is the most significant factor on any team. Strong pitching can outweigh other major flaws.

I don't have to remind anyone of how important pitching proved for the Mets that season. That's on record.

We beat the Cubs in the first

game of the series on July 8, pulling out the game with three runs in the ninth inning after going in trailing, 3–1. After the game Santo blasted Don Young, the Cubs center fielder, for not having caught two fly balls that fell for hits in the ninth. Leo Durocher, the Cubs manager, also blasted Young.

The next night, Wednesday, July 9, Qualls was in center field for the Cubs instead of Young. Qualls was a rookie who had been in just a few games and was hitting around .230.

Nobody on our ball club knew anything about him except Bobby Pfeil, who had played against him in the minors. "He usually gets wood on the ball and sprays it around," Pfeil told me. "Throw him hard stuff."

There'd never been a crowd like

that to see us in Shea Stadium before. There were 50,000 people packed in there that night when I walked out to the mound. My wife, Nancy, was in the stands and so was my father. He'd come in from the West Coast and went to the ballpark directly from the airport.

I could feel the tension, the excitement, the expectation of the crowd more than I had ever sensed it before. It was stimulating, but it also put pressure on me. You couldn't help but feel it.

I was a little concerned when I warmed up because my shoulder felt tight. It took a couple innings before it loosened up, before the adrenaline started to flow and eased up the shoulder.

Ken Holtzman pitched for the Cubs and we got to him right away. Tommie Agee hit the first pitch for a triple and Pfeil doubled him in. We were ahead,

BOXSCORE

	1	2	3	4	5	6	7	8	9	R	H	E
CHICAGO CUBS	0	0	0	0	0	0	0	0	0	0	1	3
NEW YORK METS	1	2	0	0	0	0	1	0	X	4	8	0

1–0, after Holtzman had thrown just two pitches.

We scored two more runs in the second inning. I drove in one of them with a single. We got another run in the seventh when Cleon Jones hit a home run to make it 4–0.

Meanwhile I was retiring the Cubs in order, inning after inning. My shoulder felt great, and I was throwing harder than I'd ever thrown. I struck out five of the first six Cubs I faced, and when they hit the ball they hit it at somebody.

When I got Williams out to end the top of the seventh inning he was the 21st Cubs batter I'd retired in order. I hadn't walked a man. I had a perfect game going. Everybody in the ballpark knew it. Nobody on our bench said a word to me, but I knew what was going on. How could I help knowing?

Santo. Banks. Al Spangler. They all went out in the eighth. With every out the crowd roared — 50,000 people yelling, roaring, cheering me, pulling for me to pitch a perfect game. Three outs to go. I felt I could do it.

The hitters in the ninth were Hundley, Qualls and then a pinch hitter for the pitcher. When I went out to the mound I heard a roar greater than the ones before. Everybody was standing up and cheering.

Hundley squared away to bunt. He laid it down, but I got off the mound quickly and threw him out. Just two out to go!

Qualls stepped in, a left-handed hitter. The first time up he'd hit a fastball to the warning track in right field. The next time he'd hit a curve ball very sharply to first base. I was trying different pitches on him, but he

seemed to get a piece of everything.

This time I tried to pitch him away, with a fastball. The ball didn't sink. It stayed up and Qualls got the bat on it. He hit a line drive to the gap between Tommie Agee in center and Jones in left. It fell for a single.

Disappointed? Of course, at the moment. I'd like to have pitched a perfect game. Anybody would.

But I got the next two batters out, Smith then Kessinger, and the game was over. I had a one-hitter and we'd won, 4–0. When I walked from the dugout through the tunnel toward the locker room I saw Nancy. She had tears in her eyes. "What are you crying for?" I said. "We won, 4–0."

I still feel the same way. Regrets? How can you have regrets about a one-hitter you pitched in the middle of a pennant race?

JOHNNY BENCH
JOHNNY ON THE SPOT

OCTOBER 11, 1972

AS TOLD TO GEORGE VASS, *BASEBALL DIGEST*, DECEMBER 1975

An effective catcher in baseball often has to frame his accomplishments within the context of his team. For Johnny Bench, who is widely regarded as the best catcher of all time, putting his team first was the most rewarding part of the game. So it isn't surprising that he doesn't mention in this memory of the 1972 NLCS that he was the National League MVP.

The 14-time All-Star who popularized the one-handed catching stance spent his entire 17-year career in Cincinnati. He was named the Rookie of the Year in 1968 and collected 10-consecutive Gold Gloves and two MVP awards. But his favorite moment was seeing his teammates' happiness after he slugged a home run to help lift the Reds to the '72 World Series. The Reds lost that Series to the freewheeling Oakland A's but would finally win in 1975 (and again in 1976).

Cincinnati faced Pittsburgh in the '72 NLCS. The two teams were the class of the National League: the Reds won the West by 10.5 games, and the Pirates won the East by 11. Bench describes the action in the final game of the series.

—SM

1972 Topps; #433

There was a time when I thought the All-Star Game in 1969 might be the game I'd remember more than any other. That's the one that was played at Washington in the afternoon because it was rained out the night before.

Willie McCovey hit two home runs and the National League won easily. But I came close to hitting a pair myself.

Mel Stottlemyre of the Yankees was the starting pitcher for the American League. We got a run off him in the first, and in the second inning I hit a two-run homer. I figured I couldn't top that for a thrill. The second time at bat I got a base hit, and the third time up I walked.

My fourth time up came in the sixth. Dave McNally of the Orioles was pitching by this time and I hit another ball well, to left field. I thought it was going into the bullpen for another homer, but Carl Yastrzemski jumped up and caught it as it was about to clear the fence.

That, to me, was the most memorable game I'd played until the National League playoffs of 1972.

We played the Pirates in that series, and there really wasn't much to choose between the clubs. We were that evenly matched.

It figured the series would go the maximum five games, and it did. The Pirates won the first game at Pittsburgh, but we bounced back and won the second. The series then moved to Cincinnati. Pittsburgh won the third game, but we won the fourth.

So it all came down to one game, which would decide the National League pennant — the winner to play Oakland in the World Series.

Steve Blass was the starting pitcher for Pittsburgh and Don Gullett went for us.

The Pirates scored a couple runs in the second inning and we got one in the third. They got another in the fourth, but Cesar Geronimo hit a home run for us in the fifth inning to cut their lead to 3–2. That was still the score when we got our last turn at bat in the ninth.

Bill Virdon, the Pirates manager, brought in his best reliever, Dave Giusti, to pitch to us in the ninth. I was the first batter. Giusti had struck me out in the ninth inning of the third game when the score was the same, 3–2, and no doubt Virdon remembered that. I know I did.

In a situation like that, when all you've got to do is get three outs and you've got a pennant, you go with your best, and there was no doubt

BOXSCORE

	1	2	3	4	5	6	7	8	9	R	H	E
PITTSBURGH PIRATES	0	2	0	1	0	0	0	0	0	3	8	0
CINCINNATI REDS	0	0	1	0	1	0	0	0	2	4	7	1

Giusti was that for Virdon. He'd saved 22 games and won seven that season for the Pirates. He'd been in plenty of tough situations.

I felt strong, though, and I told Pete Rose, "I'm going to hit one. I feel it."

I was swinging from my heels. I just felt so good and was seeing the pitches so well that I knew I was going to hit the ball hard unless Giusti made a super pitch. On the third pitch he threw a palm ball right over the plate, like the one he threw to strike me out the last time we faced each other. This time I hit it.

I can't describe the feeling as I saw the ball soar out there. I knew it was gone. I knew the game was tied and that we'd win it.

I don' t remember running around the bases. All I know is I was going around them, making sure I stepped on each one and home plate.

When I headed for the dugout I can't really explain to anyone how I felt, not just because I'd hit the home run but because of what it meant. I was just so happy to see the guys' smiling and laughing at me when I ran into the dugout. I got more enjoyment out of seeing their happy faces than I did of anything I accomplished.

They all had a part in this because you share everything with the guys on your team. They are the people you're working with for eight months. You love all of them and to see them happy is more satisfying than anything else.

They knew now we'd win the game, though my home run had only tied it, 3–3. But you get a feeling, and you know it's going to happen one way or the other.

It came quickly. After I hit the homer Tony Perez and Denis Menke singled and we had runners on first and second with nobody out. We were getting to Giusti, and after he threw two balls to Geronimo, Virdon brought in Bob Moose to pitch.

Geronimo hit a fly ball to deep right, and George Foster, who was running for Perez, took third after the catch. With one out and a runner on third, all we needed was a good fly ball to win the pennant.

The next batter, Darrel Chaney, popped out and Foster was still on third with two out. Now Hal McRae was batting and we needed a hit to win, or we thought we did.

Moose got the count to 1-1 and his third pitch hit the edge of the plate, bounced away from the catcher and Foster scored the pennant-winning run. I can still see that ball bouncing off the plate and Foster crossing home.

No matter how long I live that moment will stick in my memory.

> I GOT MORE ENJOYMENT OUT OF SEEING [MY TEAMMATES'] HAPPY FACES THAN I DID OF ANYTHING I ACCOMPLISHED.

KEN GRIFFEY

SEVENTH HEAVEN

OCTOBER 22, 1975

▽

AS TOLD TO GEORGE VASS, *BASEBALL DIGEST*, APRIL 1987

Crammed with emphatic moments, the 1975 World Series has stood the test of time and is still regarded as one of the best World Series ever played. Which memory stands out most depends on your perspective. For many, it's Carlton Fisk's semaphore, urging his 12th-inning homer in Game 6 to stay fair. For Ken Griffey, of course, it was the next game: few people remember that he scored the winning run.

It was Griffey's first season as a full-time player with the Reds. He spent the first nine years of his MLB career in Cincinnati, nearly winning a batting title in 1976, and returned there after stints with the New York Yankees (1982–1986) and Atlanta Braves (1986–1988).

In this story the 19-year major leaguer isn't referred to as Ken Griffey Sr. because his Hall of Fame son didn't make his major league debut until two years after this story was originally run. To a younger generation Griffey is best remembered for starting in the Mariners outfield beside his son on August 31, 1990. It was the first time a father and son played on the same team at the same time. Two weeks later they hit back-to-back home runs.

—SM

Ken Griffey of the
Cincinnati Reds in 1975.

1975 Topps; #284

Outfield

KEN GRIFFEY

I'm very proud of the championship rings I earned with the Reds during the big years of the mid-1970s. We won the World Series in '75 and '76 and we had a great team. I take a lot of pride in what we accomplished winning those pennants and beating the Boston Red Sox and then New York Yankees in those two Series.

That was a part of my career I'll never forget. It was important to me at the time, and it's important to me so many years later. I was a Red for 12 years, and I often think of all the great players we had on that club — guys like Pete Rose, Joe Morgan, Tony Perez, George Foster and the rest. When you've been part of something like that you never forget.

Besides, I'm a National Leaguer at heart. I'm not saying I regret the years I was with the Yankees, but I've always been in a National League frame of mind. I like the way they play the game. I grew up in Donora, Pennsylvania — hometown of National Leaguer Stan Musial. Maybe that's why I've always taken special pride in my hitting. Not that I'm comparing myself to Musial, but I've had success most years.

I've never won a batting championship, but I've come about as close as you can get without winning it. In a way, I guess, that brings me up to one of the games I won't forget, though I didn't play the entire game.

Going into the final day of the '76 season I was leading the National

League in hitting with .337. Bill Madlock of the Chicago Cubs was right behind me at .333.

Our manager, Sparky Anderson, decided to keep me out of the game to protect my average. It's not what I wanted, but he was the boss. So I was on the bench when the game against Atlanta started.

Somebody reported that Madlock had gotten hits his first four times at bat in Chicago, so he was ahead of me in the batting race, .339 to .337. Sparky put me into the game as a pinch hitter, but I struck out twice and that was it. I finished at .336, Madlock at .339.

That was a personal disappointment, but you really can't feel bad for too long about hitting .336.

Besides, we went on to win the National League pennant against the Philadelphia Phillies that year and then swept the Yankees in the World Series, which made up for any disappointment I might have felt about not winning the batting title.

BOXSCORE

	1	2	3	4	5	6	7	8	9	R	H	E
CINCINNATI REDS	0	0	0	0	0	2	1	0	1	4	9	0
BOSTON RED SOX	0	0	3	0	0	0	0	0	0	3	5	2

Even still, the most memorable moment in my career is the 1975 World Series against the Red Sox. Some people have said it was one of the greatest Series ever played, and maybe it was.

There were a lot of big moments right from the beginning when Luis Tiant shut us out (6–0) in the first game.

The first game in Cincinnati was the most controversial one. That was the third game of the Series, and we went into the bottom of the 10th tied, 5–5. Cesar Geronimo led off with a single. Ed Armbrister attempted to sacrifice and bunted the ball in front of the plate. When Carlton Fisk, the catcher, grabbed the ball he threw to second trying to force Geronimo. The ball sailed into center field and Geronimo went to third.

The Red Sox were all over the plate umpire, Larry Barnett, claiming Armbrister had interfered with Fisk. But the play stood and Geronimo eventually scored the winning run.

Another highlight was the sixth game at Boston. I've seen that replay of Fisk hitting the winning homer in the 12th inning a dozen times on TV, and it was one of the biggest moments in World Series history, though not for us. Still, we won the Series, and that's what counts.

Game 7 at Fenway Park is the one I'll never forget. There's no thrill to match winning the World Series and knowing you've been a part of it.

I had a good game. I got a single in the third inning, then a walk in the seventh, which led to the run that tied the game at 3–3. Pete Rose drove me in with a single.

We went into the ninth still tied, and by this time Jim Burton, a left-hander, was pitching for the Red Sox. All I had in mind was to get on-base, so I waited him out and got a walk to lead off the inning.

Geronimo sacrificed me to second and I went to third on an infield out by Dan Driessen. After Rose walked,

Joe Morgan whopped a grounder through the infield for a single and I scored the lead run.

Morgan was an outstanding hitter, but I don't think he ever got a bigger hit than that chopper through the infield. I know I never scored a bigger run. That made it 4–3, and we hung on to win the game and the World Series.

I can't think of a bigger moment than that one.

> I TAKE A LOT OF PRIDE IN WHAT WE ACCOMPLISHED WINNING THOSE PENNANTS AND BEATING THE BOSTON RED SOX AND THEN NEW YORK YANKEES IN THOSE TWO SERIES.

ROBIN YOUNT

BREWING SOMETHING SPECIAL

OCTOBER 3, 1982

AS TOLD TO GEORGE VASS, *BASEBALL DIGEST*, JULY 1986

Robin Yount was 30 years old when he said, here, that he didn't like playing center field as much as shortstop. But after two shoulder surgeries in less than two years he had to make the move. He couldn't have known, though, that three seasons after this recollection appeared in Baseball Digest *he would become just the second American League player (Hank Greenberg did it in the outfield and at first base) to be named league MVP at two different positions.*

Yount played his entire 20-year career with the Milwaukee Brewers, who made only one World Series appearance — the one they earned in this memory — during his career. For the first 11 years he didn't play any position except shortstop, and for the final eight he played only center field. In the transition year of 1985 he played the other two spots in the outfield, as well as center.

Yount led the American League in hits, doubles, extra bases hits and total bases in 1982. In Milwaukee's seven-game loss to the St. Louis Cardinals he hit .414 and became the first player ever to have two four-hit games in one World Series.

—SM

Robin Yount hits during the first game of the 1982 World Series.

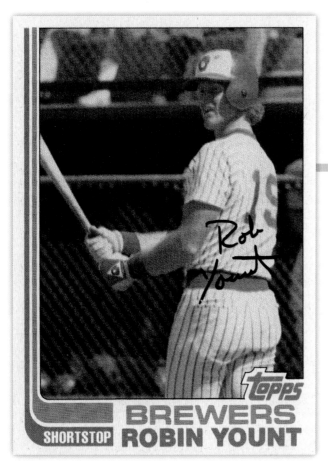

1982 Topps; #485

SHORTSTOP BREWERS ROBIN YOUNT

L ooking back it's difficult to believe I've been around as long as I have, since I came up to the Brewers in 1974. I don't feel that old, and I guess I'm not. I hope to go a long time yet.

We've been up and down in that time, both the Brewers and me. But teams run in cycles. When I first came up we were at the bottom and we worked our way to first in 1982. Now we're down again, but I can see us climbing with the talent we've got on our club.

There's no doubt in my mind that the high point of my career came in '82 when we won the American League pennant at Milwaukee. There have been other high spots, of course, but '82 stands head and shoulders above everything else. When your team wins, this game seems a lot easier.

I can't say that baseball bas been as much fun as it should be the past couple seasons. After the '84 season I had arthroscopic surgery on my shoulder and I thought that would clear things up. But the shoulder just got worse to the point I couldn't throw more than a few feet without it hurting. I had surgery on it again in '85 to remove bone spurs and calcium deposits. It really worked wonders, though I'll never again be able to throw as well as I could before the problem.

I can't say I enjoy playing the outfield, where I am now, as much as I did playing shortstop. Playing in the field keeps you a little far from the action and maybe it's a little more difficult to concentrate there, but I'll do anything I can to help the team and keep playing.

The thought of having another season like we had in '82 is all the motivation I need. It's the kind of season every player dreams about, and I don't mean from an individual standpoint. We won the East Division title, won the AL playoffs and got into the World Series.

A lot of things stand out about that season, right down to the seventh game of the World Series, which we lost to the St. Louis Cardinals. That just adds another incentive. Every player wants to be on a World Series winner at least once. The thing about being in a World Series is that once you've been there you want to go back. It's worth the hard work and effort.

But when I sit back and think about it four years later, the one game that stands out the most was the final game of the regular season, against the Baltimore Orioles.

OCTOBER 3, 1982
BOXSCORE

	1	2	3	4	5	6	7	8	9	R	H	E
MILWAUKEE BREWERS	1	1	1	0	0	1	0	1	5	10	11	1
BALTIMORE ORIOLES	0	0	1	0	0	0	0	1	0	2	10	1

The way things were going during most of the '82 season you'd never have figured it would come down to the last game. We really got rolling after the All-Star Game, and by late August we had something like a seven-game lead. I think Baltimore was in second place at the time.

But then Rollie Fingers, who was our stopper out of the bullpen, got hurt and our lead started to dwindle. All the same we had a three-game lead over the Orioles going into the last series of the season: four games in Baltimore.

Anybody who knows anything about baseball knows a team can't afford to relax in that kind of situation, even if all they need is one game out of four. When you're the team that's chasing, you figure all you've got to do is win four straight and that doesn't seem all that much. Well, Baltimore almost did it.

The series opened with a double-header. We figured we had a good chance of getting a split, but we didn't. The Orioles won both games and were just a game out.

The next day was what really hurt. They pounded us, 11–3, and tied us for first place with a game to go and everything hanging on that game.

It seemed like the Orioles had everything going for them. They had Jim Palmer starting and, to top it off, it was going to be Earl Weaver's last game as Baltimore's manager because he had announced he was retiring after the season.

Our starter was Don Sutton, whom we'd traded for late in the season. Like Palmer he was a veteran who'd been in tense situations before. Neither team could have wanted a different pitcher out there.

The ballpark was jammed that day, not only because a division title was riding on that last game, but because of Weaver. He got a tremendous ovation when he came out on the field. If emotion and crowd enthusiasm could

have won the game the Orioles would have breezed by us.

I don't think I've ever felt much more tension and excitement than I did at the start of that game. Everything we'd been working toward all season was on the line. So, you force yourself to concentrate and that's what I did when I came to bat in the first inning. I don't remember the exact count, but Palmer came in with a pitch about waist high. I hit it out to put us ahead, 1–0. We picked up another run in the second inning, and my next turn at bat, in the third, I hit another home run.

Sutton was working a good game for us, and by the ninth we were leading, 5–2. A five-run burst in the top of the inning put the game away. We won 10–2 to go to the league championship series.

It wasn't the two home runs and the triple I hit that made it stand out for me. It was the fact we won the division title. You never forget a game like that.

PAUL MOLITOR
GIVING PRAISE

OCTOBER 12, 1982

✕

AS TOLD TO GEORGE VASS, *BASEBALL DIGEST*, OCTOBER 1991

Paul Molitor was still a Milwaukee Brewer when he reminisced, here, about his first appearance in the Fall Classic. Milwaukee had beaten the California Angels in a best-of-five series in the 1982 ALCS and then took on the Cardinals in the World Series. The Brewers had the Cards on the ropes, with a 3-2 series lead, but lost the final two games in St. Louis.

Molitor continued to have personal success with the Brewers, including his 39-game hitting streak, which remains the fifth longest in modern baseball history. But he longed for another shot at a World Series title, and he'd have to leave Milwaukee to get it.

His chance would come two years after recounting this story to George Vass. After 15 seasons with the Brewers he signed in Toronto, which was coming off its first championship in franchise history. The Blue Jays were reloading for another run and added Molitor to an already potent lineup. The move paid off for both. The Jays won the 1993 World Series and Molitor was named Series MVP. He scored the winning run on Joe Carter's famous walk off homer.

—SM

Paul Molitor tags home after his fifth-inning inside-the-park home run during Game 2 of the 1982 ALCS.

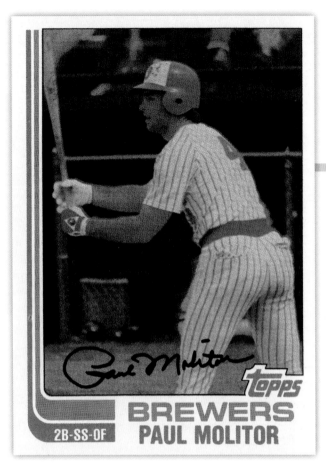

1982 Topps; #195

2B-SS-OF
BREWERS
PAUL MOLITOR

It is hard to believe I've been in the major leagues all these years. To look back and realize I've played almost 15 years, that's really amazing.

I've been hurt a lot, and every spring the thing I wish for the season is good health. It can be pretty frustrating to get hurt so often. But experience teaches that you can't always avoid the things that happen.

Getting hurt is aggravating at first. The thought of going through rehab is terrible. But when it happens you stop and think how fortunate you are to be where you are and for what the game has given you and what God has given you. And then there are all the people who have helped along the way. Denis Menke, who was my manager when I started in professional baseball at Burlington (Midwest League, 1977) after signing out of college, is a person I'm very grateful to have worked with.

Denis changed my batting style, and that made me a much better hitter. He made me more of a stand-up hitter. I sacrificed a little power with the style change, but I made more consistent contact. Denis encouraged me to close up my stance more and he taught me to hit to right field more consistently. I would never have guessed I could hit to right field as much as I have done since.

There have been a lot of other people who have helped me along the way, and experience also has been a big help. After a while you learn how to do things the right way and how to make the most of whatever natural ability you are blessed with.

I've played a lot of positions with the Brewers over the years — shortstop, second base, center field, third base, you name it. I used to joke that I'd better start working on my slider in case I was needed in the bullpen.

I'm not complaining. I'm just glad to help wherever I can. And if my switching positions helps the club to win, I'm all for doing so.

Naturally the most memorable times are when you win a division title or a league pennant and get into the World Series. I wish it could have happened more often for us in Milwaukee, but the one time we did win the American League pennant in 1982 does stand out.

It was one of those seasons you dream about having as a team, with an exciting pennant race, a comeback win in the playoffs and a spot in the World Series.

OCTOBER 12, 1982

BOXSCORE

	1	2	3	4	5	6	7	8	9	R	H	E
MILWAUKEE BREWERS	2	0	0	1	1	2	0	0	4	10	17	0
ST. LOUIS CARDINALS	0	0	0	0	0	0	0	0	0	0	3	1

That year we took a three-game lead into the final series of the regular season, with four games to go in Baltimore. The Orioles won the first three games, so we went into the final game tied for first place with Baltimore and the division title riding on the outcome.

Fortunately, Don Sutton, whom we'd gotten in a trade just a few weeks earlier, pitched a great game for us, and Robin Yount had a terrific day at bat with two homers and a triple, We won, 10–2, to clinch the division title.

We had to pull it out in the playoffs, too, when we lost the first two games to the California Angels. But we came back and won the next three to win the American League pennant. That final game, in Milwaukee, was something I'll never forget. It was just a tremendous thrill, winning a pennant in front of your own fans.

We played the St. Louis Cardinals in the World Series, and there were a lot of high spots, games and plays that stand out from it even now. I just wish we could have won it, but I guess it wasn't meant to be.

Even then, there was one personal highlight that will always stand out for me, something I'll remember long after I retire from playing.

That came in the first game against the Cardinals when I got five hits after grounding out my first time at bat. Getting five hits in your first World Series game is something that's got to be among the highlights of your career.

But we didn't win the Series and that hurt. Still you always hope for another chance and maybe that'll come yet, before I hang it up.

Of course, there have been a lot of other memorable games in my career, and I'll be able to sit back and think about them when I retire. Some of them came during the 39-game hitting streak that I had in 1987, and I guess

the most memorable one came in the game that finally ended the streak.

I'd gone hitless against Cleveland at County Stadium on August 26, 1987, in my first four times at bat. The score was 0–0 in the bottom of the 10th inning, and I was in the on-deck circle waiting for another turn at bat when Rick Manning singled to drive in the winning run. The streak was over. I guess it was meant to be 39, not 40 or any other number.

When I headed for the dugout, the crowd got on its feet and gave me an ovation. That was probably the most emotional moment of the streak.

That streak was a great experience and I was thankful to have had the opportunity. The fact that it's one of the longest in the history of the game makes you realize you're very fortunate to have it.

I've always enjoyed the game, and I'm grateful I've had the opportunity to have so many moments to remember.

RICK SUTCLIFFE
CHANGE FOR THE BETTER

SEPTEMBER 24, 1984

AS TOLD TO GEORGE VASS, *BASEBALL DIGEST*, APRIL 1992

The seven-game 2016 World Series between the teams with the two longest championship droughts in baseball — the Chicago Cubs (108 years) and the Cleveland Indians (68 years) — was memorable for every baseball fan. But it was particularly poignant for Rick Sutcliffe, who is now a network baseball analyst. He pitched for both clubs in 1984, the season he recalls here.

Sutcliffe was having a dismal year in Cleveland, both on and off the field, when he was traded to Chicago in June of '84. But the Windy City and Wrigley were exactly what the doctor ordered. After going just 4-5 with the Indians Sutcliffe went a sizzling 16-1 as the Cubs chased their first National League pennant since 1945.

The good times kept rolling to start the postseason as Chicago went up 2-0 in a best-of-five series against San Diego, but the Padres swept the next three at home to prolong the Cubs' championship drought.

Sutcliffe threw the ceremonial pitch before the first game of the 2016 NLCS between the Cubs and Dodgers, another of his former teams. He also threw the first pitch ever at Camden Yards, the Baltimore gem that changed modern stadium architecture.

—SM

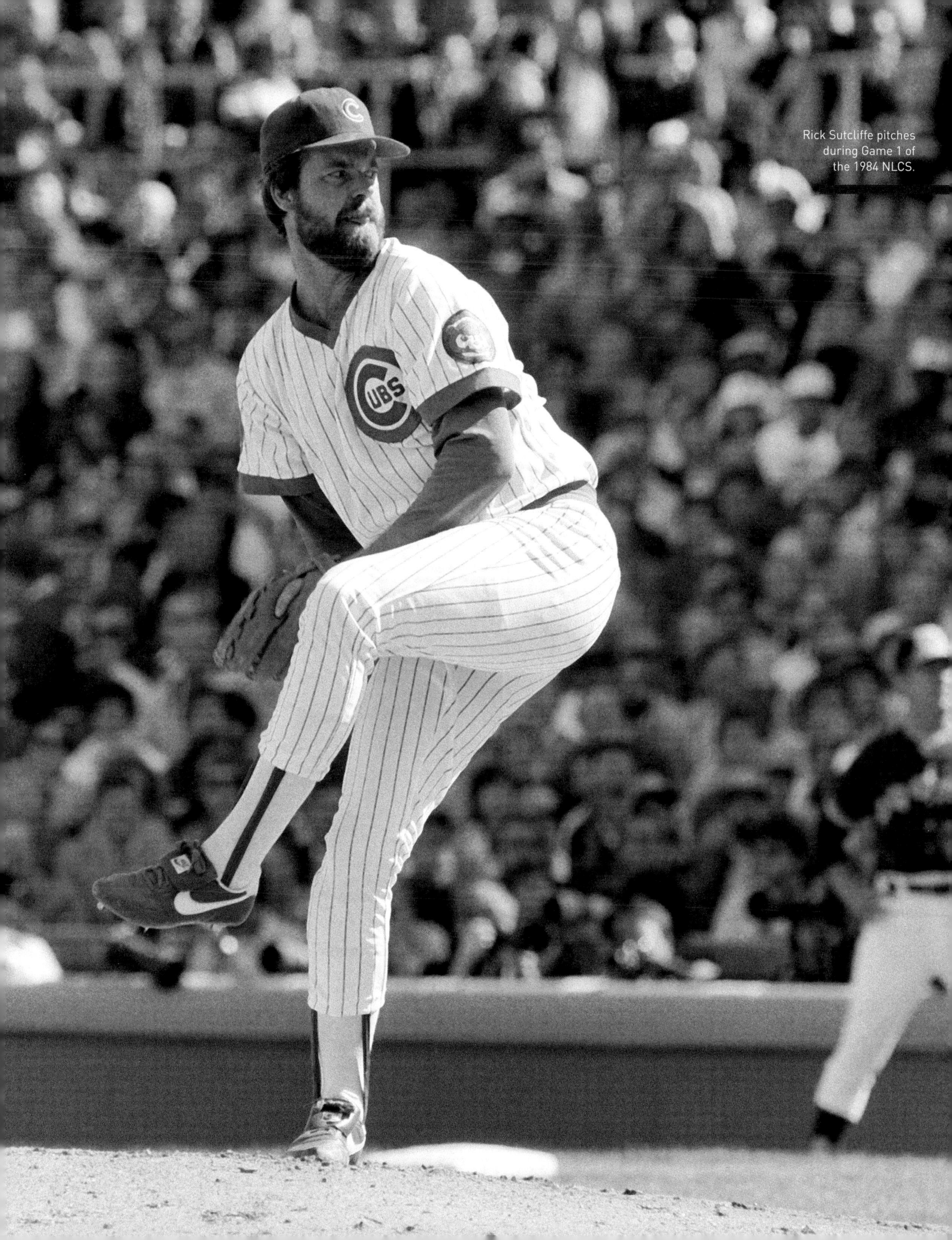

Rick Sutcliffe pitches during Game 1 of the 1984 NLCS.

1984 Topps; #285

RICK
SUTCLIFFE   P

The greatest thing that ever happened to me in baseball was when I was traded by the Indians to the Cubs early in the 1984 season.

It opened everything up for me. It made it possible for me to have a great season, to contribute to winning a division title and to set my career on a course that would satisfy my personal goals and repay the community and the fans. After all, the fans are the ones who support a team and make it all possible. You can't ever forget that.

I've always felt strongly that a ballplayer owes a great deal to the fans, and I think that the greatest gift I have as a baseball player is to be able to touch people and make a small difference in their lives, whether it's by meeting them or contributing to causes.

I was really having a miserable time in Cleveland early in the '84 season. I was sick, suffering with root canal problems and I had to have surgery. I wasn't able to eat solid food for two weeks. I lost 17 pounds, but I had to keep pitching. I had no strength. My fastball was terrible, but the club said it needed pitchers and they couldn't put me on the disabled list.

When the trade was made I was coming back into form. It was a nice boost to go from a team that was 20.5 games out of first place to another that was 1.5 games in front. I made up 22 games overnight.

Looking back, joining the Cubs was a dream. I had the time of my life and so did the entire team. The fans and the support they gave us had a lot to do with it. They hadn't had a winner in such a long time that they really really appreciated what we were doing, the way we were playing hard, the way we were winning. I've never been around an atmosphere of excitement like we had that year — it was really amazing. We could be five runs down, and if the leadoff man got on-base 40,000 people were up on their feet giving us a standing ovation, trying to get something going. And it worked. It definitely helped us. By August we were in first place to stay and we won the division title.

I am proud to have been part of that. I had my best season, and it's unbelievable that I was 16-1 with the Cubs after the trade.

I don't want to make it seem like it was an individual thing. I was just part of that. It takes a team to win. The Cubs were in first place when I got there and had unbelievable comeback

BOXSCORE

	1	2	3	4	5	6	7	8	9	R	H	E
CHICAGO CUBS	1	1	1	0	1	0	0	0	0	4	10	0
PITTSBURGH PIRATES	0	0	0	1	0	0	0	0	0	1	2	3

ability that year. There were a lot of outstanding players, like Ryne Sandberg, Gary Matthews, Keith Moreland, Jody Davis, and a lot of other guys who contributed.

Naturally any number of games stand out for me that year.

One, for sure, is the game in which we clinched the division title in Pittsburgh.

We were in first place by five or six games at the time, and we were anxious to put it away because even in the last week of a season a lead like that can get away from you.

I made the start against the Pirates and I felt pretty good and strong warming up. Still, throwing well in warm-up doesn't guarantee a good start in the game. I think it really helped that we scored a run in the first inning on a double by Sandberg and a single by Matthews. When you've got a lead out of the gate — even just one run — it gives you a boost of confidence to go out there and pitch your game.

This time I had all my stuff — fastball, breaking ball, changeup — and it was one of the best games I ever pitched. I think I only faced 28 men and gave up just two hits. We scored a couple more runs in the early innings and eventually won, 4–1.

We'd won the division championship. It's a feeling I have a hard time describing — and how the fans back home in Chicago reacted. That was great. They hadn't won anything in so long.

The other game that stands out, of course, is the first game of the playoffs against San Diego at Wrigley Field.

After I retired the Padres in the first, Bob Dernier led off for us with a home run. Before the inning was over, Matthews hit another home run and we had a 2–0 lead. We scored three more runs in the third inning when I led off with a home run. That was a big thrill for me.

We went on to win, 13–0. We won the next game and it looked like we

had a good shot at getting into the World Series. But the Padres won the next three games in San Diego. It was one of the greatest disappointments of my career, not getting into the World Series.

We won the division again in '89 in Chicago, but this time San Francisco beat us in the playoffs.

I wish we could have brought a World Series to Chicago. I guess it wasn't meant to be. But I've got nothing but the fondest memories of my years with the Cubs, and I always will treasure the time I spent with them.

> . . . THE FANS ARE
> THE ONES WHO
> SUPPORT A TEAM
> AND MAKE IT ALL
> POSSIBLE. YOU CAN'T
> EVER FORGET THAT.

OZZIE SMITH
'THE WIZARD' MAKES MAGIC

OCTOBER 14, 1985

AS TOLD TO GEORGE VASS, *BASEBALL DIGEST*, JUNE 1992

A quarter-century after he recalled this home run to Baseball Digest, *very little of the artificial turf Ozzie Smith had adjusted to as his era's best shortstop remained in major league stadiums. He was a 15-time All-Star, largely because of his magical hands in the field, but even his gaudy defensive statistics don't capture him. You had to see his acrobatic play with your own eyes.*

Smith hit only 28 home runs in his entire 19 years in the majors, most of those with the Cardinals. He never hit more than six in any season, which coincidentally came the same year he hit the lone postseason homer of his career. But he made it count — a walk off ninth inning solo blast at Busch Stadium to give St. Louis a 3-2 series lead over the Los Angeles Dodgers in the NLCS. The Cardinals went on to win the pennant two days later in Game 6 when Jack Clark hit a home run in the ninth. Smith was named series MVP.

When Smith retired he had won 13 straight Gold Glove Awards and held the major league record for career assists and double plays by a shortstop. He was aptly nicknamed "The Wizard."

—SM

Ozzie Smith celebrates after hitting the game-winning homer in the ninth inning to defeat the Los Angeles Dodgers 3–2, and take a 3–2 lead in the 1985 NLCS.

1985 Topps; #605

I pride myself on defense. To me it's an art, and like any other art you have to study all the time to make the most of your skills, to be consistent and to improve all you can. You can never stop learning, never let up and be satisfied with the way you're doing things.

Being able to adjust, to learn, to improvise is all part of playing defense well. To me, being a jazz player is a lot like being a shortstop. In jazz you have to know something so well that you can improvise, be free to create something different, yet something that follows naturally.

Six or seven years ago you didn't see many guys throwing on the run. Now it's something they do all the time.

Some guys even throw off the wrong foot if they don't have the time to adjust—it's the only way they can beat the baserunner.

Of course, the artificial turf has a lot to do with it because the ball is scooting a lot quicker on the ground. It doesn't give you as much time to field the ball, cradle it, get a good motion and take a good look. You've got to make the play now or it's too late. It has to be bang-bang.

I've worked at my art all my life. I've never had the greatest arm in the world, but I've always taken pride in being fast and accurate with my throws. Even as a kid I'd practice by the hour making throws, picking a spot to hit and trying to come as close to it as I possibly could.

You could say it's all about adjustment and making the most of the skills you were given. It's also about being as entertaining as possible, because part of baseball is making people enjoy watching you play. You want to give them their money's worth, and most of all you want to make sure you don't cheat anybody — especially yourself — by being less than you can be.

I've been fortunate to be on a team for a long time, one that's been in three World Series. It makes a difference when you play with people for an extended period of time, because you become aware of where everybody is. You know what to expect, you play together like a team and you put the individual things aside.

When we won we had good defense. A lot of people may tend to underestimate defense in baseball, but it's just as important as any other aspect of the game. Good defense means taking momentum away from the other team,

BOXSCORE

	1	2	3	4	5	6	7	8	9	R	H	E
LOS ANGELES DODGERS	0	0	0	2	0	0	0	0	0	2	5	1
ST. LOUIS CARDINALS	2	0	0	0	0	0	0	0	1	3	5	1

the team at bat, and giving it to your team. It keeps you in the game.

Over the years I suppose I could think of a lot of defensive plays I took pride in, some that stood out for me. But the important thing about it is that they weren't by accident. They were the result of hard work, of being able to improvise in certain situations.

But when people ask me about the games that stand out for me in my career, it's something else. It's a team thing, like clinching a division title, winning a pennant or winning a World Series.

Nothing can top winning the Series, so when we beat the Milwaukee Brewers in 1982, that was one of the highlights of my career. And although it's a great achievement just to play in the World Series it always hurts to lose, so you'd have to say that among the greatest disappointments for me were the ones we lost, to Kansas City in '85 and Minnesota in '87.

There's no doubt that one playoff game I'll never forget was the fifth game of that 1985 National League Championship Series.

We went into that game tied with the Dodgers at two wins apiece. I guess you'd have to say whoever won that game would be in the driver's seat.

Fernando Valenzuela started for Los Angeles and we got to him for two runs in the first inning before he settled down. The Dodgers tied it up with a couple runs in the fourth inning, and it stayed that way, 2–2, until the ninth. When we came to bat in the bottom of the inning, the Dodgers sent in Tom Niedenfuer to pitch. He got Willie McGee to pop out to start the inning and then got ahead of me, 1-2, on the count.

I'm not sure what the next pitch was, but I saw it and I hit it well. It hit off the concrete pillar above the right-field wall for a home run and we'd won the game, 3–2.

I guess you'd have to say that I was an unlikely hero because I don't hit that many home runs. But I'm a better offensive player than I'm given credit for.

And the way I look at it, the defense puts the offense in a position to win. So when a player known for his defense can contribute a little offense, that's a plus.

> YOU CAN NEVER STOP LEARNING, NEVER LET UP AND BE SATISFIED WITH THE WAY YOU'RE DOING THINGS.

GARY CARTER
EXTRA EFFORT

OCTOBER 15, 1986

AS TOLD TO GEORGE VASS, *BASEBALL DIGEST*, JULY 1991

Gary Carter's career began in the outfield, but he quickly found his home behind the plate. He became an excellent defensive catcher who knew how to handle himself with a bat in his hands as well. While dedicating himself to his pitchers he still managed to hit .262 with 324 homers and 1,225 RBIs in his 19-year career.

The long-time Expo was the first Montreal player inducted in the Hall of Fame. He spent the first 12 years of his career with the Expos, many of them losing seasons, until he was traded to the New York Mets in 1984. It was with the Mets that he finally won the World Series, in 1986.

It was the highlight of his career. But the game that stood out the most for Carter was the 16-inning affair in Houston that got the Mets there.

Perhaps because of the drama that followed it in the World Series, the 1986 NLCS between the Mets and Astros is one of the most overlooked pieces of entertainment in the past half-century. It didn't escape Carter's attention though, especially Game 6 in the Astrodome, which became the longest postseason game in baseball history at that point.

—SM

Gary Carter, center, celebrates with relief pitcher Jesse Orosco on October 14, 1986 after Carter won Game 5 of the 1986 NLCS with a 12th inning walk off single.

GARY CARTER
N.L. ALL STAR

1986 Topps; #708

A lthough it wasn't my ambition at first to be a catcher, I'm glad I became one. I don't think there's another position in which you're so involved in each game. It gives you so much opportunity to use your head as well as your athletic ability.

I played outfield, first and third, but I realized I could make it quicker as a catcher. There's always a big demand for catchers. Even when the Expos brought me up as an outfielder (1974) I continued to work on my catching, and they moved me there permanently in my third year.

It was a conscious decision on my part to concentrate on catching, and I'm thankful I did.

With all the responsibilities a

catcher has, I'm surprised some of them hit as well as they do. A catcher usually doesn't get to work as much on his hitting as other players do, though I always tried to get in my swings.

Often you're tied up working with a pitcher or talking to the manager or pitching coach about something going on with the staff. A catcher is always involved with many more things on the club than with himself.

It's the same during a game. You're concerned more with your pitcher or the situation that's developing. You're in the middle of every play, every pitch. The whole game is right in front of you and you're concentrating for nine innings on everything, fighting off all sorts of distractions. It's a real challenge to keep the game in focus.

In the early years, with Montreal, the highlight would have had to come in 1981, the year we had the long strike. That was the year we played two playoff series: one for the division championship and the other for the National League pennant. Although we lost the pennant to the Dodgers, just getting into the postseason was a thrill.

Above everything, though, would have to be the years with the Mets, especially 1986 when we came back to win the World Series over the Boston Red Sox.

There are a lot of things in that Series that stand out in my mind, and I'm sure in a lot of other people's as well. Nobody's going to forget that sixth game when we came back from being down two runs with two out and nobody on-base in the 10th inning and the Red Sox one out away from wrapping up the World Series.

I'd hit two home runs in the fourth game of the Series, but the single I got

BOXSCORE

	1	2	3	4	5	6	7	8	9	10	11	12	13	14	15	16	R	H	E
NEW YORK METS	0	0	0	0	0	0	0	0	3	0	0	0	0	1	0	3	7	11	0
HOUSTON ASTROS	3	0	0	0	0	0	0	0	0	0	0	0	0	1	0	2	6	11	1

in Game 6 with two out and nobody on-base in the 10th was even more important. It kept us alive and we went on to win that game and then the seventh.

I don't know how you can top the thrill of winning a World Series. That stands by itself.

But of all the games I've played I can't think of any one that would quite match the final playoff game in '86 against the Houston Astros in the Astrodome. I don't know if there's ever been a better ball game.

Every game in that series was a struggle. The day before, the fifth game had gone 12 innings. We won it, 2–1, and what made it especially memorable for me is that I drove in the winning run with a single in the 12th after going 1-for 21 in the playoffs up to that point.

That put us ahead three games to two in the series and gave us a chance to wrap it up in the sixth game. We were especially anxious to do that because we knew the Astros would have their best pitcher, Mike Scott, ready for the seventh game. He'd shut us out, 1–0, in the first game and beaten us, 3–1, in the fourth game, too.

In Game 6 the Astros got out front early, 3–0, but we tied them with three runs in the ninth inning. Nobody scored again until the 14th, when we pushed a run across, but Billy Hatcher hit a home run in the bottom of the inning to tie the game.

When we scored three runs in the top of the 16th to take a 7–4 lead it looked as if we were in good shape. But it wasn't that easy. Jesse Orosco was pitching for us, and before we knew it the Astros had two runs across, men on first and second and Kevin Bass, a dangerous hitter, at bat with two out.

I knew Orosco didn't have much left, but we were going to stay with him to pitch to Bass. At that point Keith Hernandez (first baseman) came to the mound with Orosco and myself and said, "Whatever you do, Gary, don't let Jesse throw Bass a fastball." I wasn't about to, and Jesse knew what he had to do.

Jesse reached back for everything he had and struck out Bass on six straight breaking balls. We won the game, 7–6, and wrapped up the pennant.

I can't think of any game I've played in that was better than that one. It lasted almost five hours. It just drained every one of us out on that field.

It's a game no one will ever forget.

> A CATCHER IS ALWAYS INVOLVED WITH MANY MORE THINGS ON THE CLUB THAN WITH HIMSELF.

JACK MORRIS
HOMETOWN HERO

OCTOBER 27, 1991

AS TOLD TO GEORGE VASS, *BASEBALL DIGEST*, JULY 2014

Prior to the brilliant matchup between the Minnesota Twins and Atlanta Braves in 1991, only 13 pitchers had thrown complete-game victories in Game 7 of the World Series. Jack Morris would become the 14th — and the first to have to go into extra innings to do it.

His opponent for the Series finale was John Smoltz. Through seven innings neither pitcher had allowed a run. Morris survived a bases-loaded scare in the eighth, and his teammates managed to drive Smoltz from the game in the bottom of the inning, even though they didn't score.

It was still scoreless when Morris took the mound for the 10th. He'd already thrown 118 pitches on just three days rest, and he went out and threw eight more to retire the side, paving the way for Gene Larkin's pinch-hit RBI that won the Series in the bottom of the inning.

It was one of the greatest World Series ever, with five of the seven games decided in the last at-bat, four on the final pitch, and it was a testament to the career-long workhorse approach of Morris, who was named World Series MVP to cap his only season with his hometown Twins.

—SM

1991 Topps; #75

JACK MORRIS

There was no question in my mind that we were going to win that game. I was pitching and I wasn't going to let us lose. I was totally confident about what was going to happen, and I felt like I could pitch all night if I had to.

Some people take this the wrong way, but I think if you're a competitive athlete, especially a professional athlete, you dream of being in that kind of situation. And when the opportunity arises, you love being out there in front of the whole world. I was very much aware that there were millions and millions of people watching all around the world, and they were all focused on the guy holding the baseball on the mound.

To be on that stage at that moment when the whole world is watching, if you don't live for that moment as a baseball player, then you probably have the wrong job. You might be in the wrong business. I wanted to be that guy in that moment. Maybe that sounds wrong to some people, but I loved that feeling.

Smoltz and I were both pitching well through seven innings. In the top of the eighth, with one out and two on, manager Tom Kelly came to the mound. He didn't come out to see how I was feeling or take me out of the game. He just wanted to talk about who we should face. First base was open and the Braves had David Justice and Sid Bream coming up, so we walked Justice intentionally to load the bases for Bream. He was thinking fly ball, I was thinking ground ball.

When Bream hit a grounder to Kent Hrbek for a 3-2-3 double play, it was deafening in the Metrodome. Simply deafening. You could feel it shake. During the Series I kept thinking to myself that I'm in it with the fans and there's no way we're going to lose. I wasn't going to let them down. I wasn't going to let that happen.

I retired the Braves in the ninth, and we got two men on in the bottom of the inning but didn't score. I was going back out, period. I was pitching the 10th. They would have had to tear my uniform off to keep me from going back out.

I got the Braves in order again in the 10th and in our half of the inning Dan Gladden opened up with a double. When he scored from third on Gene Larkin's single to deep center off Alejandro Pena, I remember the noise, the jubilation, the feeling you have for your teammates. It's all just pure joy. It was such a wonderful baseball game — it was fitting for the Series to end with such a brilliant game. It shouldn't have been any other way.

I felt like winning the Series was for us — for Minnesota — and I was so proud and happy to be a part of it. It was never a "me" thing on that team or in that city. It was always "we" — and together we won that World Series.

OCTOBER 27, 1991
BOXSCORE

	1	2	3	4	5	6	7	8	9	10	R	H	E
ATLANTA BRAVES	0	0	0	0	0	0	0	0	0	0	0	7	0
MINNESOTA TWINS	0	0	0	0	0	0	0	0	0	1	1	10	0

DAVE WINFIELD

WINDING UP A WINNER

OCTOBER 24, 1992

◊

AS TOLD TO GEORGE VASS, *BASEBALL DIGEST*, OCTOBER 1993

Dave Winfield had 18 career RBIs in post season play, but none came close in importance to the bouncing two-run double he hit down the left-field line to give the Toronto Blue Jays the first World Series victory by a team not located in the United States. Winfield, three weeks past his 41st birthday, became the third-oldest player, after Pete Rose and Enos Slaughter, to record an extra-base hit in the Fall Classic. It was the only World Series extra-base hit of Winfield's career.

Winfield is one of just five players to be drafted by three professional sports (baseball, basketball and football, which he didn't even play in college), and he is the only person to be drafted by four different pro leagues. (The American Basketball Association was going head to head with the NBA in 1973, his draft year.)

In a 2004 ESPN poll Winfield, who never played a game in the minor leagues, was chosen the third-best all-around athlete, in any sport. And somewhat fitting of such an athlete, Winfield was born on October 3, 1951 — the day Bobby Thomson hit the Shot Heard 'Round the World.

—SM

Dave Winfield of the Toronto Blue Jays celebrates with a teammate after winning the 1992 World Series.

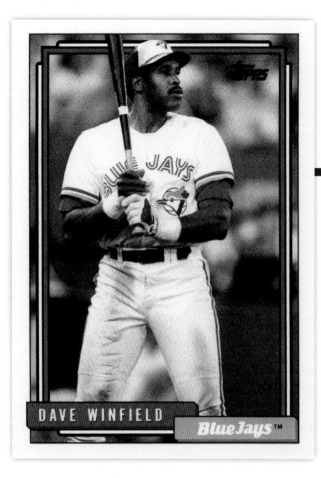

1992 Topps; #130T

DAVE WINFIELD Blue Jays™

W hen you start out, you never think you'll play for 20 years, but it just happens. And the way you play the game and the way you look at the people you come in contact with change along the way. As your career evolves, your perception of yourself and the way people perceive you change.

One thing I'm sure of is that I've never regretted choosing baseball. I had options and I'm happy I chose baseball. It's made for a unique experience that I really wouldn't change.

One of the finest things about baseball is that you meet a lot of people in the game, a lot of characters. I mean that in a positive way, because I'm talking about people who were fun to be around, teammates you could respect

and enjoy being with. Like Kurt Bevacqua when I was with the San Diego Padres. He was a loud and boisterous guy with a deep voice and a big laugh, and he had a sense of humor. He was a real practical joker.

One time we had a young player who liked to pop off, even though he hadn't accomplished all that much. Kurt was the leader and he and his pals stretched him out and covered him with molasses, sunflower seeds and powder. You didn't hear all that much from the guy after that.

There were also Gaylord Perry, Dave Kingman, and some others you remember from the Padres, but we could never put it together in San Diego. We had some good players, but not enough to win. The mix wasn't

there. They were mostly players who were either too young or too old.

So when the opportunity came for a change and I signed with the New York Yankees, I was very happy about it. There were so many more people on the team who could help you out. I knew that we had a chance to win.

It was great to win the pennant that first year (1981) and get into the World Series. It's a unique experience, your first World Series, and you feel good about having contributed to getting there.

It was a shame I didn't have a better series (1-for-22), but you have your ups and downs in this game and you can't brood on them. You always look forward to having another chance. I had no idea it would take so long.

What really hurt in New York, though, was the antagonism (from Yankees owner George Steinbrenner). I had some good years, but there was no appreciation. When I hurt my back and had surgery and had to sit out a

BOXSCORE

	1	2	3	4	5	6	7	8	9	10	11	R	H	E
TORONTO BLUE JAYS	1	0	0	1	0	0	0	0	0	0	2	4	14	1
ATLANTA BRAVES	0	0	1	0	0	0	0	0	1	0	1	3	8	1

whole year in 1989, the Yankees gave up on me. They had no faith I could come back.

When they traded me to the California Angels in 1990 they did me a great favor. It revived my career, and after 17 years I really enjoyed what I was doing.

I enjoyed the people I was with: Dave Parker, Wally Joyner, Bert Blyleven. It was a quiet clubhouse, except maybe for Parker. He loved to needle everybody. When we were both in the outfield, they compared us to bookends, in right field and in left field. We had similar styles of play and we weren't as young as most of the others.

It was a lot of fun and I enjoyed myself more than ever after all those years in New York.

When I signed with the Toronto Blue Jays in 1992, I was in a situation that suited me perfectly. We had a good mix of players, a lot of ability and the philosophy of the game that I like: work hard and have fun, but manage yourself and be ready to play.

I'd played with Cito Gaston when he was still a player in San Diego, and I really had to respect him as a manager. He's intelligent. He knows how to use his team, which is a manager's greatest strength. And he won with it.

To get another chance in the World Series after all those years, you can't ask for more than that. And to win it — that's the ultimate experience for a baseball player.

There were a lot of highlights in the sixth game of the World Series against the Braves in Atlanta, but two in particular stand out for me.

I started the game in right field and we had a chance to win the Series right there because we were up three games to two going in. About the seventh inning, the manager has to start thinking about defense, and Cito asked me how I felt, how my legs were. We had a 2–1 lead, and he thought about putting someone out there for defense. I told him I felt fine, that I had no problems.

In the bottom of the eighth Ron Gant led off for the Braves with a sinking liner, and I had to come in for it and make a sliding catch. I was glad that I could show Cito it wouldn't have been right to take me out for defense. I could still make plays.

It also gave me the opportunity for the high point of my career: the hit that won the Series.

When I came to bat against Charlie Leibrandt in the 11th we had men on first and second and two out. I said a couple extra prayers. I never wanted a hit more than I did that one.

When I hit it past third base for a double to drive in two runs, it was a load off my shoulders. It was one measly hit, but it was the biggest hit of my career. It gave us a 4–2 lead, and we were able to hang on and win it 4–3.

It was great to be on a winner and to be a leader. Being on that team was the most fun I've had during the course of a year with a club.

ADDITIONAL CAPTIONS

Above: Atlanta Braves catcher Greg Olson celebrates with pitcher John Smoltz as the Braves clinch the National League West on Saturday, October 5, 1991.

2–3: Johnny Podres pitches for the Brooklyn Dodgers during the 1955 World Series, which the Dodgers won for their first title in franchise history.

5; 146–147: Milwaukee's Robin Yount celebrates with the crowd after the Brewers' Game 5 win in the 1982 World Series. Yount's home run in the seventh inning broke the game open for the Brewers.

8: Los Angeles Dodgers pitcher Fernando Valenzuela is doused with champagne by teammate Tom Niedenfuer after the Dodgers won the 1981 National League title.

72: Sandy Koufax of the Los Angeles Dodgers pitches to Chris Krug of the Chicago Cubs in the top of the ninth inning, en route to his perfect game in 1965.

106: Boston's Carlton Fisk jumps on home plate after hitting his famous 12th inning walk-off homer in Game 6 of the 1975 World Series.

INDEX